Nubble Light

CAPE NEDDICK LIGHT STATION, YORK, MAINE

By Jeremy D'Entremont

CIDER MILL
PRESS

BOOK
PUBLISHERS
KENNEBUNKPORT, MAINE

13-Digit ISBN: 978-1-60433-778-5
10-Digit ISBN: 1-60433-778-8

This book may be ordered by mail from the publisher. Please include $5.99 for postage and handling. Please support your local bookseller first!

Books published by Cider Mill Press Book Publishers are available at special discounts for bulk purchases in the United States by corporations, institutions, and other organizations. For more information, please contact the publisher.

Cider Mill Press Book Publishers
"Where good books are ready for press"
PO Box 454
12 Spring Street
Kennebunkport, Maine 04046

Visit us online!
cidermillpress.com

Cover design by Cindy Butler
Interior design by Chris Russell
Typography: Apollo MT, Mrs. Eaves, Neutraface, Baskerville, Dakota
Image Credits: The Author: Jeremy D'Entremont; Douglas Ax, pg. 59; Jim Burrill, pg. 60; U.S. Coast Guard on pp. 60, 98, 100, 110; Steve Reed, pg. 61, 99-109; Rose Labrie, pg. 75; William O. Thomson, pg. 76, 88, 126; Herb Carpenter, pg. 81, 136; Barbara Finnemore, pg. 83; Debbie Jones, pg. 84; Bob Trapani, Jr. pg. 86, 87; Connie Small, pg. 94; American Lighthouse Foundation, pg. 94; Richard Winchester, pg. 111; Elinor DeWire, pg. 126; Friends of Flying Santa, pg. 128; Richard Beauchesne, pg. 144; Deb Cram, pg. 148; All illustrations used under official license from shutterstock.com

Printed in China

1 2 3 4 5 6 7 8 9 0
First Edition

(photo by the author)

York Me Nubble Light

Introduction ～～～～～～～～～～～

Nubble Light is as pretty a lighthouse as you'll ever see, but it also has another tremendous advantage. Unlike so many lighthouses that are perched in remote locations, often far offshore, Nubble Light is easy for the average person to see. It is, however, on an island. You can drive to Sohier Park in York, Maine, for a breathtaking view of the lighthouse—but you can't get on the island, even though it's less than 200 feet away.

Some people believe that's part of Nubble Light's charm. You can get tantalizingly close, but you can't quite touch it. In any case, this is indisputably one of the world's best-loved lighthouses and an icon of the rocky Maine coast. With the possible exception of Portland Head Light, Nubble Light has been utilized more than any other lighthouse in art and advertising.

A red fishing shack in Rockport, Massachusetts, is known as Motif #1 because it's said to be painted by artists more than any building in the United States. The esteemed maritime historian Edward Rowe Snow once called Nubble Light "Motif #2." In terms of the sheer number of visitors and the volume of photos taken, Nubble Light and Portland Head Light would have to be at the top of the list. I would not venture to say which of them is first. Suffice it to say that anyone traveling to Maine with even a passing interest in lighthouses needs to visit both.

I first viewed Nubble Light some 30 years ago, right around the time of its 1987 automation. Since then, I have visited Sohier Park to view the lighthouse literally hundreds of times, often with tour groups. I always tell people that I never get tired of the place, and I mean that sincerely. No two visits are the same. The sea, sky, and wildlife constantly change; the light plays off the buildings in new ways. As much as I love it in summer, when the pink and white beach roses are in bloom at Sohier Park and the grass around the lighthouse is greener than green, I think I love Nubble best when it has a frosting of new snow in winter. It's like sweet icing has been spread on the proverbial cake.

March 2005. (photo by the author)

Acknowledgments

There are many people I want to thank for their help with this book. Historians Jane Molloy Porter, Elinor DeWire, and J. Candace Clifford all generously shared their research materials from their own study of this and other lighthouses. Matt Rosenberg, modern-day lighthouse keeper and goodwill ambassador for Nubble Light, was very helpful and supportive. Herb Carpenter kindly shared photos and information on "Captain Burke's Store." Barbara Finnemore and her daughter, Norma Clark, graciously shared material on Keeper Fairfield Moore.

Steven B. Reed, son of Coast Guard lighthouse keeper Bruce Reed, shared information about his family as well as a treasure trove of photos. Richard Winchester, son of Coast Guard keeper David Winchester, was also a great help.

The Old York Historical Society was an important research source, and I especially want to thank Pat FitzGerald for her kind assistance. Elizabeth Stevens, librarian at the Bangor Public Library, took the time to go through the library's collection of lighthouse articles in the *Maine Coast Fisherman*.

I want to express my gratitude to all the staff and volunteers who work at Nubble Light and everyone at the York Parks and Recreation Department. Without them, none of this would be possible.

I owe a large debt to William O. "Bill" Thomson, who has been a friend for many years. His knowledge of Nubble Light is second to none. Bill Thomson's work over the years, along with the writings of Clifford Shattuck, Jane Porter, Edward Rowe Snow, Jeffrey Patten, Rose Labrie, and others, laid the foundation for this book.

Others I wish to thank, in no particular order: Bob Trapani, Jr., executive director of the American Lighthouse Foundation; James W. Claflin of Kenrick Claflin & Son Nautical Antiques; the staffs of the National Archives, the Library of Congress, and the U.S. Coast Guard Historian's Office; the U.S. Lighthouse Society, particularly Executive Director Jeff Gales; Dolly Bicknell; and Brian Tague, president of Friends of Flying Santa.

As always, the Cider Mill Press team has been a joy to work with. Many thanks to John Whalen, editor Mike Urban, designers Chris Russell and Cindy Butler, and also Brittany Wason. And, of course, my wife, Charlotte Raczkowski, is deserving of more gratitude that I can express. Ever since I quit a "real job" nearly 20 years ago to become a full-time lighthouse bum, she has been nothing but supportive.

—**Jeremy D'Entremont**
  Portsmouth, New Hampshire
  April 2017

July 2008. (photo by the author)

Some Historical Background

To lighthouse buffs and lovers of the New England coast, the word "Nubble" instantly conjures images of a postcard-perfect, gleaming white lighthouse on a rugged, rocky island surrounded by the deep blue ocean, accented by the whoosh of waves, the screech of soaring gulls, and the hubbub of happy tourists from around the world. Although the official name of the lighthouse in government records is Cape Neddick Light Station, few people use that name. To most, it's Nubble Light, or simply the Nubble.

Where did this odd but catchy name originate? Before we determine the answer to the question, let's begin with some historical context.

Before the arrival of European settlers, Agamenticus was the name native people used for the area of the southern Maine coast around what we now know as the York River. That old name is retained in the name of nearby Mount Agamenticus, now a public park

SOUTHWARD, ON NUBBLE-POINT, THE LIGHT;

BY DAY A STURDY SHAFT OF WHITE,

BY NIGHT A GLOWING CRIMSON EYE,

BY WHICH THE COASTWISE VESSELS HIE.

—*William Hale, "Cape Neddick Harbor"*

that offers expansive views that span from the ocean to the White Mountains to Boston. European settlers, who first arrived in 1624, changed the name to Bristol, after Bristol, England, in 1638.

Sir Ferdinando Gorges, the lord proprietor of Maine who is sometimes referred to as the "father of English colonization in North America," re-named the area yet again. He called it Georgeana (or Gorgeana, after himself) and made it the capital of the Province of Maine. In 1642, Georgeana became the first incorporated city in North America. There were about 200 non-native residents by 1650.

Later, after Gorges's death, Maine came under the governance of the Massachusetts Bay Colony. The town of York—named for York, England—was carved out of a segment of Georgeana. York was incorporated as a town in 1652, making it the second oldest town in Maine after Kittery.

A raid by the local Abenaki Indians, the so-called Candlemas Massacre, largely decimated the town in January 1692. York again flourished in the second half of the 18th century, as it became a center for significant trade with

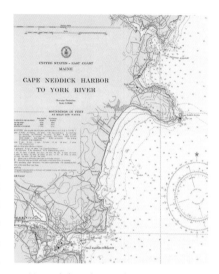

Nautical chart showing the Cape Neddick area and the location of the Nubble. (collection of the author)

the West Indies. Trade diminished after the Embargo Act of 1807, but the town eventually rebounded with fishing, shipbuilding, and the export of lumber playing major roles, along with an increasing emphasis on tourism after the Civil War.

York is large area-wise, with 55 square miles of land and 77 square miles of water within its boundaries. The town is divided into four sections, or villages: York Village, York Harbor, York Beach, and Cape Neddick. As usually defined, Cape Neddick stretches for about 10 miles along the coast—from Bald Head Cliff near the border with Ogunquit in the north, south to York Harbor. The area known as York Beach, which consists of two beaches, is contained within Cape Neddick.

The fairly straight coastline of Cape Neddick is interrupted in its midsection by a peninsula, known historically as Cape Neck (or Cape Neddick Neck), jutting out about a mile to the east. Just off the tip of this peninsula is the rocky little island known as the Nubble. The name "Neddick" seems to have been derived from a Micmac Indian word that was used for small rocky islands in New England and eastern Canada. Thus, it would appear that the name used by native people for the island was eventually used for the surrounding area.

It's believed by many historians that the explorer Bartholomew Gosnold, who sailed from Falmouth, England, on the bark *Concord*, met with local American Indians on the island in May 1602. He dubbed it "Savage Rock." One of Gosnold's crew, John Brereton, wrote:

From the said rock came towards us a Biscay shallop with sail and oars, having eight persons in it, whom we supposed at first to be Christians distressed. But approaching us nearer we perceived them to be savages. These coming within call, hailed us, and we answered…They spoke divers Christian words and seemed to understand much more than we, for want of language to comprehend. …These much desired our longer stay, but finding ourselves short of our purposed place, we set sail westward, leaving them and their coast.

Captain John Smith, the English explorer and soldier, sailed along the coast of Maine to Massachusetts Bay in 1614. The map he published in 1616, based on his explorations, was the first to bear the name "New England" for the region. It isn't clear if Smith stepped ashore in the area of Cape Neddick, but his map showed a roughly accurate depiction.

Some historians have credited a member of Smith's crew for naming the Nubble (often spelled "Knubble" in records before 1900), but other

Captain John Smith, from an old English print. (collection of the author)

Some confusion creeps into the picture as many local residents in the present day refer to the entire Cape Neck peninsula as the Nubble. For the purposes of this book, the name Nubble refers to the island and its lighthouse only.

ROCK FORMATIONS ON THE NUBBLE

Sometimes a rock is more than just a rock. New Hampshire had its famous Old Man in the Mountain, and the Nubble has several celebrated formations chiseled by nature into its rocky contours. According to the historian William O. Thomson, the locations are as follows:

• George Washington's Profile, on the north side of the island.

• The Devil's Oven, formed by a jagged, deep crevice near the lighthouse tower. It was given its name by one of the keepers, according to Thomson.

• Pulpit Rock — On the island's northeast side, a formation that is said to resemble a church pulpit.

• Whale Rock — Also known as the Sea Serpent, on the beach near the boathouse.

historians have disputed this. The location was not named on Smith's map.

Whether or not Smith or a member of his crew first applied the name, it seems to be simply a carryover of an old English word to the New World.

The word "nubble" is defined as "a small knob or protuberance" by the Random House Dictionary; it's the diminutive of knob or nub.

Washington Profile, Nubble Island, York, Me.

The rock formation known as Washington's Profile, from an old postcard.
(collection of the author)

It was recorded that the area near the Nubble was being used for the pasturing of goats around 1643. In the years between the early English explorations and the establishment of its celebrated lighthouse, the Nubble's chief claim to fame seems to have been as a popular place for duck hunting. The 1880 book *History of York County, Maine*, informs us that the Nubble was "a celebrated ducking-ground of sportsmen, widely known as such in several states."

The Call for a Lighthouse

The earliest call for a light-house on the Nubble dates back to around 1807, but the idea was shelved after some debate. Almost three decades later in 1834, U.S. Representative Edward Kavanagh, who later served about a year as governor of Maine, introduced in Congress a petition of "sundry inhabitants of the State of Maine, praying for an appropriation for the erection of a light-house on York Nubble." Three years later, after repeated requests, the 24th Congress appropriated $5,000 for a lighthouse.

Several other locations were recommended for lighthouses along with the Nubble. The second part of the 1837 act directed the Board of Navy Commissioners to examine the locations and to determine whether the lighthouses were in fact needed for safe navigation.

The officer chosen to examine the locations in Maine was Captain Joseph Smith, who was the commandant of the Boston Navy Yard. Smith solicited the opinions of local merchants and mariners for his report. Green Walden, a first lieutenant in the U.S. Revenue Service, responded:

A light-house on York Nubble I consider quite unnecessary, and would serve to embarrass rather than assist the navigation. As there are five light-houses in its immediate vicinity, four of which can be seen from the Nubble in clear weather, viz: Isle of Shoals, Cape Porpoise, Boon island, and Whale's back lights. . . . . I would therefore recommend that a monument be erected on York ledge, instead of a light on the Nubble.

Twelve additional captains and merchants chimed in with their recommendation against the lighthouse:

Vessels bound up and down the coast, in clear weather, can discern the Nubble five miles in the night; and as there are no ledges near it, and no harbor where vessels can find shelter in a storm, we cannot conceive of any advantage to be derived from a light-house on the Nubble to coasters in general, or to vessels from a foreign port.

One of the arguments in favor of a lighthouse on the Nubble was that it would enable mariners to follow a route closer to shore than the one typically used at that time, which ran between York Ledge and Boon Island, a few miles offshore. Captain Smith felt that a new inner route would be more dangerous, especially with an inshore (blowing from the water toward the shore) wind.

Instead of a lighthouse on the Nubble, Smith recommended an unlighted beacon at York Ledge, which is located about two miles southeast of the entrance to the York River. He also recommended a small lighthouse at Stage Neck at the entrance to the York River, which would render the river entrance

"both easy and safe."

An unlighted monument was erected a short time later at York Ledge, designed by the renowned architect Alexander Parris, but Stage Neck never got a lighthouse. Thanks to Smith's report, the concept of a lighthouse on the Nubble would stay on the back burner for nearly a half-century.

Sea serpent sightings were often front-page news along the New England coast in the 19th century. On August 27, 1839, the *Portland Advertiser* announced that a sea serpent was seen "off the Nubble, near Cape Neddick," by the crews of several boats. The creature was said to be at least 100 feet long, with a small head like that of a snake, and to pass through the water with "extreme velocity." The boats' crews were "much alarmed and made for the land."

There have been a number of boating accidents and shipwrecks near the Nubble through the centuries, although loss of life has been rare. On February 19, 1842, the bark *William Faces* was wrecked at Cape Neddick, with the loss of eight lives. The captain

19th-century illustration of a sea serpent passing Egg Rock Lighthouse near Nahant, Massachusetts. (collection of the author)

had mistaken a light on the beach for a lighthouse, presumably the one at Boon Island.

The most memorable wreck in the area, that of the bark *Isidore*, is often cited as one of the contributing factors in the eventual establishment of the lighthouse at the Nubble. The wreck took place during a blinding snow-storm on November 30, 1842, near Bald Head Cliff, north of the Nubble.

The *Isidore* was a new ship sailing out of Kennebunk on its first voyage, carrying a cargo of hay and potatoes bound for New Orleans. Leander Foss was its owner and captain, and there were 15 men on board in all. The bark made it only a short distance from its home port. Onlookers eventually saw the wreckage from shore, but only seven bodies were recovered. Twenty children were left fatherless on that day.

THE *ISIDORE*, SOUTHERN MAINE'S GHOST SHIP

The 1842 wreck of the *Isidore* off York's Bald Head Cliff is one of southern Maine's best-known shipping disasters. Samuel Adams Drake, in his book *Nooks and Corners of the New England Coast,* described what happened on the night of November 30 during a terrible snowstorm:

> It was, indeed, as I have heard, a dreadful night, and many a vigil was kept by wife, mother, and sweetheart. At daybreak the snow lay heaped in drifts in the village streets and garden areas. It was not long before a messenger came riding in at full speed with the news that the shores of Ogunquit were fringed with the wreck of a large vessel, and that not one of her crew was left to tell the tale. The word passed from house to house. Silence and gloom reigned within the snow-beleaguered village. It was supposed the ship struck about midnight, as the Ogunquit fishermen heard in their cabins cries and groans at this hour above the noise of the tempest.

The body of 36-year-old Captain Leander Foss was never recovered, but he has a grave marker in Kennebunkport just the same.

On the stone at the town's Village Cemetery is this inscription:

> May this event God sanctify,
> And thus prepare us all to die.
> That when we leave this earthly clod,
> We may be blessed and dwell with God.

The wreck of the *Isidore* has spawned some colorful legends. On the night before the wreck, one of the crew, Thomas King, had a dream that he later related in a letter: "I looked on deck and I saw eighteen empty coffins and made inquiries what they were for. In answer to my question Capt. Foss said there was one a piece for each of the crew, but I was so poor there was none for me . . . It made an impression on my mind that something would happen to the vessel and no threats or persuasion could induce me to go to sea in her."

King was so shaken that he hid in the woods nearby, where the captain and other crewmen couldn't find him. He thus survived the disaster, as the *Isidore* ran into the rocks of Bald Head Cliff north of the Nubble.

It's been claimed that the *Isidore* appears as a phantom ship, sailing slowly along the southern Maine coast. In 1970, Edward Rowe Snow, king of New England folklore, wrote that an Isles of Shoals fisherman had seen a bark manned by "shadowy men in dripping clothes who stared straight ahead from the stations." When another vessel comes close to offer assistance, it's claimed, the *Isidore* vanishes into thin air.

In the 1970s, a fisherman out of York Harbor recovered an anchor that was thought to have come from the *Isidore*.

NUBBLE LIGHT, NUBBLE POINT, YORK BEACH, MAINE.

42827

7554. THE NUBBLE. YORK. ME.   8-14-16   Great here today   Ch...

(from the collection of the author)

Grave of Captain Leander Foss of the *Isidore*, in Kennebunkport, Maine. (photo by the author)

In spite of the *Isidore* tragedy, it would be nearly four more decades before the Nubble got its lighthouse. There was another congressional appropriation of $5,000 in 1851, partly because of the growing number of pleasure boats in the vicinity, but the project again died after some debate.

In April 1852, the schooner *Georgiana* was wrecked at Cape Neddick, and a Portland newspaper reporter offered the opinion, "Had there been a light on the Nubble, as has several times been petitioned for, the vessel would in all probability have made harbor."

The Civil War further contributed to the delay of the establishment of the lighthouse. The idea was revived in 1874, when the Lighthouse Board requested $15,000 for a lighthouse "for the benefit of the coasting trade." By that time, there were an ever-increasing number of steamships plying the coast between Boston, Portsmouth, and Portland. The request came in response to a petition from the president of the Portland Steam Packet Company and other concerned parties, which led to the Lighthouse Board's statement that "a light of the 4th order should be established at York Nubble."

The request for an appropriation was repeated in the following year, with added urgency after the September 1874 wreck of a Nova Scotia schooner, the *Emily S.*, at the Nubble. Congress made an appropriation of $15,000 in July 1876—largely through the efforts of two Maine congressmen, John Burleigh and Eugene Hale. Burleigh died in South Berwick, Maine, in late 1877, before construction of the lighthouse commenced.

There was a delay in procuring the site, which had been the property of multiple owners since 1854. With tourism in the York area on the rise, there were plans for a hotel on or near the island. The island was also a favorite campsite for duck hunters. According to the historian Jane Molloy Porter, the birdshot that was scattered in abundance on the island made it impossible for the early keepers of the lighthouse to keep chickens, as the birds ate the shot and died of lead poisoning.

The bargaining process moved the project back to early 1879, when the island was purchased for $1,500—a rather steep price at the time. The deed was recorded on February 5, 1879, and the island became federal property.

(photo by the author)

Construction and Early History of the Light Station, 1879–1900

The lighthouse and related buildings were construct-ed under the supervision of General James Chatham Duane, an engineer with the U.S. Lighthouse Board. Duane was a West Point graduate who had a distinguished career dating back to the 1840s. A proponent of cast-iron lighthouses, he once stated that such structures were "economical in cost, extremely durable, and cheap to main-tain in repair."

The cast-iron segments of the tow-er were manufactured in a Portland foundry and then transported to the is-land along with the rest of the building materials in two trips aboard the steam-er *U.S.S. Myrtle* in April 1879. The Army Corps of Engineers carried out the construction work, and the build-ings were completed by mid-June.

General James Chatham Duane. (collection of the author)

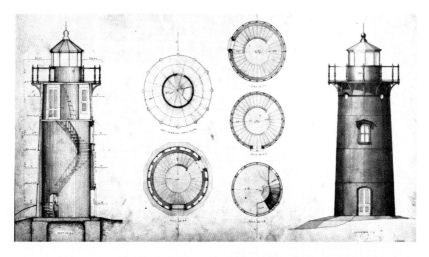

Plans for the lighthouse. (collection of the author)

A "Notice to Mariners" was published in newspapers:

On or after July 1, 1879, a fixed red light, of the 4th order, lighting 300 degrees of the horizon, will be shown from a conical iron tower, recently erected on York Nubble, Cape Neddick, Maine. The light should be seen at sea, 15 nautical miles. During thick and foggy weather, a bell will be struck by machinery, giving two blows in quick succession, followed by an interval of 30 seconds, then a single blow, also followed by an interval of 30 seconds.

CAST-IRON LIGHTHOUSES

Before the 1870s, most lighthouses in the United States were built of stone, wood, or brick. It was eventually realized that cast-iron was an ideal building material. It was light in weight, and the components could be prefabricated at foundries and easily assembled on site by small numbers of workers. Cast-iron towers could be built at relatively low cost, and they were very durable and watertight in harsh environments.

The first known cast-iron lighthouse in the world was constructed at Swansea, Wales, in 1803. The first cast-iron lighthouse in the Americas was built in 1841 at Morant Point in Jamaica. Three years later, the (continued on next page) first cast-iron lighthouse tower in the United States was constructed at Long Island Head in Boston Harbor. Today, the oldest standing cast-iron lighthouse tower in the United States is at Juniper Island, Vermont (1846), on Lake Champlain.

The lighthouse on the Nubble is one of several similar lighthouses erected in the Northeast from 1876 into the early 1880s. Similar "siblings" include Portsmouth Harbor Light in New Hampshire, Little River Light on the northern Maine coast, Stratford Point Light in Connecticut, Jeffrey's Hook Light in New York, and a few on Cape Cod—at Race Point, Chatham, Nauset, Nobska Point, and Mayo's Beach.

The style met with some resistance; writer John Albee likened the 1878 lighthouse at Portsmouth Harbor to a "length of corpulent stove pipe set on end and painted." But the graceful Italianate detailing eventually won people over, and the Nubble Light and its siblings are some of the best-loved lighthouses in the region.

Most cast-iron lighthouse towers were painted shades of red and brown in their early history using the red lead paint that was prevalent at the time. The tower at the Nubble was painted white for a time beginning in 1880, but it was soon changed back to a reddish-brown. It's been painted white since September 1, 1899, according to government documents, although some sources claim it was reddish-brown until 1902. The lantern and deck at the top of the tower have always been painted black, as is the case with most lighthouses in the United States.

Early photo of Cape Neddick Light Station, circa 1880s. (National Archives)

The spiral stairway in the tower. (photo by the author)

The *Portsmouth Journal* proclaimed the excellence of the new lighthouse on August 16, 1879: "The new lighthouse at York Nubble is one of the most substantial on our coast. It is made of cast-iron sections . . . and lined with brick from base to summit . . . . All in all, this light-house is a great institution, and must add much to the safety of the shipping on this coast."

The 41-foot tower is 14 1/2 feet wide at its base, tapering slightly to 12 1/2 feet at the lantern level. It is perched on the highest part of the island, with its light 88 feet above mean high water. The tower was lined with brick for added durability. An air space was left between the iron and brick. Some sources claim that cement was later poured to fill that space, but that would seem unlikely. The brick and cement layers would expand and

Nubble Island Light, York Beach, Me.

NUBBLE LIGHT AT NIGHT, YORK BEACH, ME.

4   Nubble Light   York Beach, Maine

(from the collection of the author)

contract at different rates, causing cracks and other problems.

A 32-step cast-iron spiral stairway, anchored to the brick walls inside the tower, leads to the watch room, where the keepers sometimes spent the night during storms to make sure the light stayed lit. From there, an eight-rung iron ladder provides access to the lantern.

Red glass panes were installed in the lantern to produce the light's red characteristic. A kerosene lamp provided the illumination, placed inside a glass, beehive-like fourth-order Fresnel lens from France. Miniature cast-iron lighthouses were placed atop the finials on the gallery railing, an architectural detail seen on only a handful of lighthouses.

The one-and-one-half-story Victorian keeper's house, painted white with delicate gingerbread trim, was situated about 50 feet north of the tower. The house was similar to a number of keepers' houses built in the same era, including the ones nearby at the White Island and Portsmouth Harbor

One of the finials on the lantern gallery railing. (photo by the author)

lighthouses. It was laid out with a living room, dining room, kitchen, and laundry room on the first floor and three bedrooms upstairs. An upstairs bathroom was later installed, but for many years the bathroom was a simple outdoor privy.

The 1879 Notice to Mariners indicated that a fog bell struck by machinery would go into operation at the same time as the light; but according to some sources, there was originally a 300-pound bell mounted on the lighthouse tower, struck by hand in response to signals from passing vessels. According to historians Clifford Shattuck and Jane Molloy Porter, a larger bell was installed on the side of the lighthouse tower a short time later.

A bell with striking machinery—installed in an open-frame, pyramidal wooden tower located just a few feet southeast of the lighthouse—went into service in 1880. The bell's original characteristic (a cycle of two blows followed by an interval of 30 seconds, followed by a single blow and another 30-second pause) was later changed to a single blow every 30 seconds.

In 1890, striking machinery from

Circa 1890s, from a postcard.
(from the collection of the author)

Maine's Pond Island Light Station was moved to the Nubble, and the characteristic was changed to a single blow every 15 seconds. An enclosed bell tower was built in 1911.

Before the light went into service, there were reportedly more than three dozen applicants for the keeper position. Leander White of New Castle, New Hampshire, who was an assistant keeper at Boon Island and would go on to serve more than 40 years in

The first fog bell tower. (from the collection of the author)

the Lighthouse Service, was appointed to be the first keeper, but he was reassigned to Whaleback Light in Kittery, Maine. Simon Leighton of York subsequently accepted the job. He operated the light during some preliminary tests in June 1879 but had to resign because of illness.

Nathaniel H. Otterson of Hookset, New Hampshire, was appointed keeper at the end of June 1879 at $500 yearly—plus an allowance of $30 for fuel. According to some sources, a temporary keeper served for a few days until Otterson arrived on July 5.

Nubble Light was a tourist attraction from the very start. Just two months after the light went into service, a writer for a Concord, New Hampshire, newspaper reported that he had been part of a group that had visited the Nubble. "Our party was courteously received," he wrote, "and shown over the premises. The outlook from the lantern of the lighthouse is grand."

Soon after the light went into service, a writer in the *Portsmouth Chronicle* complained that it was no help to mariners entering York Harbor,

This photo from the late 1890s shows two lighthouse keepers in the foreground. It's believed that the man on the left is Brackett Lewis, keeper at the Nubble, and the man on the right is William C. Williams, longtime keeper at Boon Island Light, a few miles offshore. (from the collection of the author)

although it did benefit vessels traveling along the coast. The new light meant a quicker inside route and shorter voyages. This was not viewed so positively by some of the local fishermen, who complained that the larger vessels now skirting the coast presented a new danger for them, and they had to be continually on the lookout for large vessels that came "rocking and tumbling through the waves," according to the *Portsmouth Chronicle*.

During the years that the Nubble was a staffed light station, shipwrecks in its vicinity were rare. There was a notable one in early June 1898, while Brackett Lewis was keeper. A two-masted schooner, the *Florence E. Tower*, was transporting lumber from Machias, Maine, when it lost its rudder and sprang a leak, leading to its grounding near the Nubble. The captain and three crewmen abandoned the ship and went ashore in a dory.

A number of additions and improvements were carried out in the late 1800s. A boathouse was added to the station in 1888, along with a boat slip and winch. In the following year, the boat slip was extended and access to it was improved by the removal of boulders, and a new set of stairs from the boathouse to the upper part of the island was added.

In 1898, a telephone line connected the light station to York Beach, funded by an appropriation for national defense during the Spanish-American War.

(photo by the author)

1900 to World War II

The boat slip was lengthened and improved in 1900, when about 50 large boulders were removed. The boathouse has been replaced twice over the years. Most recently, the great blizzard of February 6–7, 1978, washed out the boathouse, and it had to be rebuilt.

THE OIL HOUSE

During the early days of lighthouses in the United States, the oil used to fuel the light (whale oil, lard oil, and various other oils) was often stored in the lighthouse tower. Some lighthouses were constructed with attached oil room and workroom structures.

By 1890, kerosene (also known as mineral oil) was the primary fuel being burned in all but a few lighthouses in the United States. The volatile nature of kerosene necessitated the construction of separate oil houses, which were usually built of fireproof materials, such as brick, stone, iron, or concrete. Congress issued a series of small appropriations for the construction of separate fireproof oil houses at each lighthouse station.

The 1902 Instructions to Light-Keepers manual stated, "All mineral oil belonging to the Light House Service shall be kept in an oil house or a room by itself. The oil house shall be visited daily to detect loss by leakage or otherwise, and every precaution taken for the safe keeping of the oil." Installation of these structures began in 1888 and was completed by about 1918. The Nubble's oil house, built of brick, was constructed in 1902.

After lights were converted to electricity and oil was no longer required, the structures were used for other purposes, often paint storage. In the case of the Nubble's oil house, a generator for backup power was installed in the building. The generator came in handy when lightning knocked out electrical power at the lighthouse during a storm in June 1956.

Only a very small number of oil houses were painted red like the one at the Nubble. The Coast Guard painted it white in the early 1960s, but there were many complaints about the change, and the York Chamber of Commerce requested that it be changed back to its original red. The Coast Guard complied in the following year, and it's been red ever since.

The distinctive red oil house was built in 1902. There is also a large storage shed on the island, built at an unknown date. The shed isn't seen in the earliest photos of the station, but it was in place by the 1890s.

Brackett Lewis served the longest stint of any keeper, from 1885 to 1904. A 1904 article described a visit with a group of friends to the Nubble shortly before Lewis retired: "The lighthouse keeper came to his door and in response to our eager beckoning waved back, and started down to his little boat landing. My friend being unaccustomed to boating was somewhat startled when her side of the boat settled in the water. She clutched me and—dare I say it—shrieked."

On their arrival at the island, the party was greeted by two barking dogs and the keeper's wife, Sybil Lewis. The writer noticed a table inside the keeper's house where photographs of the lighthouse and other local scenes were displayed and were available for

The oil house. (photo by the author)

purchase. Near the foot of the stairs in the lighthouse were the lamps that were used inside the lens, equipped with red globes that produced the light's red characteristic.

After climbing to the lantern, Sybil Lewis removed the daytime chamois covering from the Fresnel lens so the group could see it. "We never put our hands on this," Sybil explained. From the lantern, the writer admired the "magnificent view of the surrounding country."

A 1905 photo by John A. Gould of the lighthouse and fog bell tower. (from the collection of the author)

Postcard view of a keeper transporting visitors in the "Nubble ferry," circa early 1900s. (from the collection of the author)

Circa 1915 postcard. (from the collection of the author)

Circa 1930s postcard showing the 1911 fog bell tower. (from the collection of the author)

The keeper's wife next showed the fog bell to the group. Entering the bell tower and taking the cover from the machinery, she explained, "This goes by clockwork. We put the handle on here, and we wind it up so. On foggy or stormy days, we keep this ringing both day and night." She demonstrated the mechanism, and the sound of the bell was so loud that the building shook.

FOG SIGNALS

Lighthouses and fog signals have gone hand in hand for hundreds of years. When fog and other factors obstruct visibility to the point that mariners cannot see the light, fog signals (also known as sound signals) provide an auditory aid to navigation that helps the mariner determine his position. For many years, the primary fog signal was the fog bell; various types of horns and sirens gradually replaced them.

The use of fog bells dates back to the 1700s in Europe and to the 1820s in the United States. Like the lights, the bells had precise characteristics that enabled mariners to easily differentiate them, such as one blow every 10 seconds.

The bells were made of bronze and could be as heavy as 5,000 pounds. The earliest fog bells were sounded manually, but automatic striking machinery was eventually developed. At many locations, pyramidal fog bell towers were constructed, with the striking machinery inside.

A white, enclosed, pyramidal tower replaced the original skeleton-frame bell tower at the Nubble in 1911. It was reported that the keepers at Boon Island Light Station—six miles away—could hear the Nubble's bell at times. It took the keeper 20 minutes to wind the striking mechanism, and it had to be rewound every four hours. Most keepers took to partially winding it every half-hour. When the mechanism was wound, weights would rise inside the tower. As the weights gradually fell, they drove a hammer. The hammer passed through a slot to strike the bell, which hung on the side of the tower.

The Coast Guard tore down the bell tower in 1961. It was knocked down to the seaward side of the island and burned. The bronze bell in service at that time went to the Coast Guard station in South Portland, Maine, and remained in storage for a while. A committee was formed in York to preserve the bell. It was led by Thomas Eastwood, owner of the nearby Nubble Cove Cottages, and his wife. The group was able to obtain ownership of the bell, and it was donated to the trustees of Short Sands Park. It was dedicated in its new location, by a shade pavilion at Short Sands Beach, in the summer of 1963.

Today, an automatic electric foghorn, mounted on the lantern gallery of the lighthouse tower, remains in use at the Nubble. The latest in the evolution of fog signal technology is the MRASS (Mariner Radio Activated Sound System), meaning a mariner can activate the horn with the use of a VHF radio.

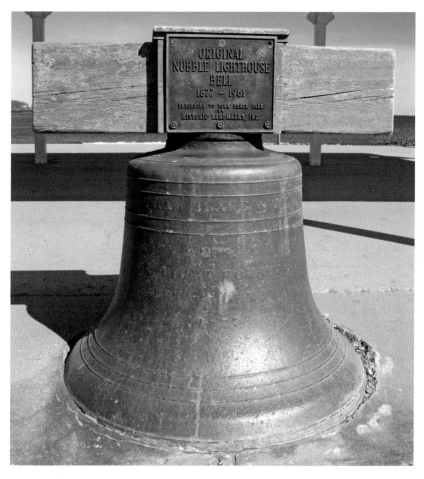

Fog bell from the Nubble, now on display at Short Sands Beach in York. (photo by the author)

THE FRESNEL LENS

The Fresnel lens, named for the French engineer Augustin Jean Fresnel (Freh-NEL) was one of the most important inventions of the 19th century. The lens was perfected in the early 1820s and was quickly adopted in many countries, but it took a few decades before the technology was adopted in the United States. The multiple glass prisms that made up the lens directed the light from a source inside the lens into a powerful horizontal beam. Some of the lenses were equipped with round flash panels, or "bull's eye" panels, that created a flash as the lens rotated around a light source.

Most Fresnel lenses were manufactured in France; a smaller number were made in England and the United States. They were constructed in various sizes, or orders. First-order lenses, the largest and most powerful, were as tall as 12 feet and were made up of hundreds of individual prisms. First-order lenses were used at primary seacoast lights in areas of major shipping. The sizes used in the United States went from first-order down to small sixth-order lenses. There were also a very small number of "hyper-radial" or "hyper-radiant" lenses used, even larger than first order.

Nubble Light's present fourth-order Fresnel lens was manufactured in 1891 by F. Barbier in Paris. The original 1879 lens was manufactured in France by Sautter-Lemonnier. The present lens was moved from another station in 1928 after the original lens was damaged in an explosion.

NUBBLE LIGHT, YORK BEACH, ME.

(from the collection of the author)

The Nubble Light, Cape Neddick, Maine (off York Beach).

Light House, York Beach, Me.

(from the collection of the author)

The covered walkways that connected the lighthouse to the keeper's house and the house to the fog bell tower were added in 1911, the same year the bell tower was rebuilt. The walkway between the tower and house—30 feet long and about four feet wide—came in very handy during storms, eliminating the need for the keeper to go outside when traveling between the lighthouse tower and his home. During some severe storms, such as the fero-cious blizzard of 1978, the wind and spray made it virtually impossible to go outside.

The base of the lens indicates that it was made by F. Barbier of Paris, France. (photo by the author)

A letter written in the 1970s by Lucy Burke Steffen, daughter of Keeper James Burke (in charge 1912–1919) to author Clifford Shattuck, revealed that the station's water supply consisted of rainwater caught on the roof and collected in a 4,000-gallon cistern in the basement of the house. Water was brought to the kitchen by the use of pumps.

The cistern was thoroughly cleaned once each year, and there were outdoor barrels to hold backup water. There

The fourth-order Fresnel lens in the lantern room at Nubble Light. (photo by the author)

was no indoor bathroom yet, just an outdoor privy. Visits to the privy must have been daunting in winter, particularly in early 1918 when the temperature dropped to 14 degrees below zero.

Lampist Joe Cocking, one of the leading experts on Fresnel lenses in the United States, inspected the Nubble lens in August 2003. (photo by the author)

WRECK OF THE *ROBERT W.*

On January 12, 1923, while Fairfield Moore was the keeper, a memorable shipwreck occurred near the Nubble, as described by William O. Thomson in *Nubble Light, York Beach, Maine.* The two-masted schooner *Robert W.* had left Thomaston, Maine, with a cargo of boxboard, headed for Lynn, Massachusetts. It had been snowing for at least three days when the schooner was sighted shortly before it ran aground at York Beach.

The only two men on board—the captain and his son—climbed the masts and lashed themselves in place with strong rope as the storm raged. The air temperature was about three below zero.

Word of the wreck spread, and multiple rescue parties headed to the scene. Howard Kelly, an assistant light keeper at Boon Island on shore leave at the time, and local resident Frank Philbrick launched a 16-foot rowboat. Their first two attempts to reach the wreck were unsuccessful, as the wind and waves drove the boat back to shore. Ice was building up on the *Robert W.*, and from shore it seemed doubtful that anyone could still be alive on the vessel. A car headlight was aimed at the schooner, but it was impossible to tell anything definitive.

A lifeboat was dispatched from the Wood Island Lifesaving Station in Kittery, but heavy seas prevented it from getting close to the wreck. Finally, Kelly and Philbrick launched their boat from a more advantageous spot. They reached the *Robert W.* and secured their boat to the schooner with a line. Captain Mitchell cut the ropes around him and fell to the deck, and he was pulled aboard the rowboat. When the captain's son, Stanley, cut himself loose, he fell into the waves. The life preserver he wore kept him afloat. Philbrick dove into the water and held tightly to Stanley.

Kelly brought the rowboat to shore with Philbrick and Stanley Mitchell hanging onto the side. Waiting arms pulled all four men from the boat when it reached shore; Stanley Mitchell and Philbrick couldn't move because their clothes were frozen solid. After a few days spent recuperating, Captain Mitchell and Stanley were able to return to their home in Rockland. The *Robert W.* was a total loss, but a mast recovered from the schooner was later used as a flagpole in front of the York Harbor Reading Room.

(photo by the author)

A government document from 1928 indicates the keeper's duties at the time, as listed by Keeper Fairfield Moore. A look at the list reminds us that the keeper's job was far more complicated than simply turning a light on and off:

•*General upkeep of the light, buildings, grounds, and fog signal.*

•*Keeping light in running condition from sunset to sunrise.*

•*After light is out, sweep and clean tower, covered way, and polish brass.*

•*Keep oil house, shed, boat house, and dwelling in condition for inspection at all times.*

•*Mow and keep grounds clean.*

•*In thick weather, snow, fog, or vapor, keep fog signal running and tower clean (at all times).*

•*Paint buildings and whitewash, when needed.*

•*Care and operation of a 4th order IOV (incandescent oil vapor) light.*

•*Care and operation of a mechanical bell fog signal.*

•*Cleaning and minor repairs of above apparatus.*

•*Cleaning, painting, and making minor repairs to structures.*

•*Keeping station records and preparing and submitting periodical reports.*

•*Observing weather conditions and aid to navigation.*

An important development in this period was the 1929 donation to the Town of York of about four acres of land on the mainland just across from the Nubble by William Davies Sohier. That donation led to the establishment of Sohier Park, which is visited by some 500,000 people yearly. The view of the lighthouse is what draws most people, but Sohier Park is also home to a busy welcome center and gift shop, and a popular restaurant is adjacent to the park.

SOHIER PARK

William Sohier, a Boston lawyer, bought about 60 acres of land opposite the Nubble in the 1870s, largely for its fine duck hunting. After his death in 1894, his son William Davies Sohier, also a lawyer and former owner of the *Boston Journal*, tried to sell the land. He described it in an advertisement, circa 1896:

About 60 acres of land at Union Bluff, York Beach. This property is located on a high bluff commanding an uninterrupted view of York Harbor, Long Beach, Concordville, York Cliffs, Bald Head, Wells, Kennebunkport, Boon Island, and the Isles of Shoals, and the most magnificent inland view in Maine. It has a sea frontage of over 1/4 mile including the Nubble Gut. It joins the estate of Gov. Sawyer and Elisha R. Brown. It is of easy access by a private way, which runs to the lighthouse, has plenty of fresh water, rocks for building, etc.

Sohier was unsuccessful in his attempts to sell the property. In 1929, he donated a four-acre segment of the property to the York Beach Village Corporation for use as a public park. The deed stated that the land would be "kept as a public park and roadway and used for the ordinary and usual park purposes and for no other uses, and not to be leased, sold, assigned, or used for any other purpose."

The transfer of the deed took place on May 15, 1929. A dedication ceremony on July 23, 1929, was attended by Sohier himself, who said he was happy that the land would be preserved as a place where "everyone was welcome to go and enjoy the wonderful views." The dedication closed with the singing of *America* by all present. Around the same time, the remainder of Sohier's property was sold as two lots to businessmen Carroll B. Trafton and Elmer R. Young.

A succession of small gift shops and restaurants has occupied Sohier Park over the years. The present welcome center and gift shop, much larger than its predecessor, was built in 2014.

There's always a crowd admiring
the view from Sohier Park.
(photo by the author)

The grounds of Sohier Park provide an ideal environment for artists. (photo by the author)

The era of civilian Lighthouse Service keepers gave way to a succession of Coast Guard keepers and their families, starting when Eugene Coleman left in 1943.

The welcome center at Sohier Park was rebuilt in 2014. (photo by the author)

(photo by the author)

The Coast Guard Era

In June 1939, President Franklin D. Roosevelt ordered that the management of lighthouses and about 30,000 aids to navigation be transferred to the Coast Guard, a consolidation that was made "in the interest of efficiency and economy." Civilian keepers were given the option of joining the Coast Guard or remaining civilians until they retired. Eugene Coleman, keeper at the Nubble since 1930, remained a civilian until his 1943 retirement.

Cape Neddick Light Station was converted to electric operation in 1938, a short time before the transition to the U.S. Coast Guard. A short time later, the heating system in the keeper's house was converted from a coal-fired burner to diesel fuel. Instead of bags of coal delivered by the crews of tenders, diesel fuel was pumped from a Coast Guard cutter to a tank near the house.

Many offshore light stations were changed to "stag" stations under the Coast Guard, with male keepers only and no families. Cape Neddick Light

Circa 1940s aerial view. Mount Agamenticus can be seen in the distance to the right. The World War II-era lookout tower is near the keeper's house. (U.S. Coast Guard photo)

Circa 1944 photo. The World War II–era lookout tower can be seen behind the walkway connecting the keeper's house and tower. (courtesy of Douglas Ax)

Station, relatively close to shore, remained a family station under the Coast Guard right up to its automation.

Having a family or couple on the island meant there was always someone there. For some years, regulations specified that the keeper or his wife were allowed to leave for up to four hours, but the other had to stay on the island. And since the wife of the keeper wasn't paid—even though she did a great deal of work—this was a more economical arrangement than having multiple male keepers.

President Roosevelt put the U.S. Coast Guard under the direction of the U.S. Navy on November 1, 1941. From then through 1945, extra Coast Guard personnel were stationed on the Nubble along with the lighthouse keeper as part of the system of coastal fortifications.

At the same time, Coast Guard boats patrolled the vicinity on the lookout for German U-boats. One of the most dramatic incidents near the Nubble in the World War II period occurred in 1943, when a U-boat sighted just to the east of the Nubble was subsequently sunk by a depth charge southwest of Boon Island.

Life returned to normal in the years following World War II. The Nubble was the scene of some filming for the 1949 movie *Lost Boundaries*, directed by Alfred L. Werker and starring Mel Ferrer. The crew was hoping for rough seas around the lighthouse, but the water was smooth as glass on the scheduled day of filming in April 1949. Af-

Circa 1949. (U.S. Coast Guard photo)

ter four days, the seas finally churned up. It was reported that the crew was working while standing in icy water that splashed up to their chests.

The official light list for the year 1950 states that the fog bell had been converted to electric operation by that time, with a single stroke every 15 seconds. Electricity meant that modern conveniences were gradually added, including television in the 1950s.

Internal Coast Guard correspondence from the early 1950s shows that some consideration was given to the idea of building a footbridge from the mainland to the Nubble. In November 1951, it was noted that the only transportation from the island was a 12-foot dory, and that landing the boat at the

Circa 1950s view. (courtesy of Jim Burrill)

island was sometimes difficult. It was felt that the improving of transportation to the island would be advantageous, as it would make it easier for families at the station, and it was also thought that family light stations were "better kept up than lights manned by single men occupying barracks."

A January 1953 letter from the Coast Guard commandant to the commander of the First Coast Guard district mentioned that the estimated cost for such a bridge was $39,200. Also under consideration was an "aerial cable tramway," with a two-passenger hand-propelled car. It was concluded that the subject required "further study and consideration."

A bridge to the island was never built, but a modified version of the "tramway" was eventually installed. Exactly when the trolley or tramway system was installed isn't clear. Steve Reed, son of Bruce Reed the Coast Guard keeper in the late 1950s, has said that he believes his father installed the first version of the system in 1959 and his family used it to move furniture off the island when they left in 1959. The original "basket" was simply a wooden box,

transported to and from the island with a manually operated pulley system.

Coast Guard Keeper Bruce Reed with his son Steve in the "tramway box" in 1959. (courtesy of Steve Reed)

The trolley system was not intended for the transportation of people—it was meant to make it easier for the keepers and families to get their groceries and other supplies across. Some families had other ideas, and people did indeed ride the trolley system across the channel at times.

The York Parks and Recreation Department added an electric motor to the trolley system around the late 1980s. The motor was in a shed on

The Nubble Island, York Beach, Me.

1398. – Cape Neddick, Nubble Light, YORK BEACH, Maine

LIGHT HOUSE, YORK BEACH, ME.

(from the collection of the author)

the mainland side, and that shed was destroyed by a severe storm in February 2013. The remains of the shed and the equipment inside, as well as the basket that hung from the cable, were removed a short time later.

February 10, 2013, just after a major winter storm smashed the shed that contained the machinery for running the tramway system.
(photo by the author)

A new version of the tramway system, with a remote controlled basket, was installed in the summer of 2017. As Mike Sullivan of the York Parks and Recreation Department has stated, the system is "very useful" for transporting building materials and other items to the island.

Later in the Coast Guard era, one of the important duties of the keepers was the reporting of the weather to the Coast Guard station in Portsmouth, New Hampshire. Every three hours,

from 6:30 a.m. to 6:30 p.m., the keeper called with a report of the wind speed and direction, the visibility, the air and water temperatures, the barometric pressure, and the wave height and frequency. The keeper also watched to make sure that the local navigational buoys were in their proper places.

For years under the Coast Guard, the light in the lighthouse was turned off 15 minutes after sunrise each morning, and then the flag was raised at 8:00 a.m. Most of the day was taken up with maintenance of the buildings; the keeper had to do all the carpentry, electrical work, plumbing, and paint-

New tramway system installed in 2017.
(photo by the author)

ing. The keeper and his family were allowed to be off the island for four hours during the day if necessary, but once the light was turned on at sunset, they were not allowed to leave until the next day.

(photo by the author)

Keepers of the Light, 1879–1987

Definitive, complete information on the keepers at lighthouses in the United States is not available from any single source.

The list below is not complete; it has been cobbled together by the author over many years of research.

Civilian Keepers

Leander White (1879 — was reassigned before lighthouse was established); Simon Leighton (1879 — resigned due to illness); Nathaniel Otterson (1879–1885); Brackett Lewis (1885–1904); William M. Brooks (1904–1912); James Burke (1912–1919); William Richardson (1919–1921); Fairfield Moore (1921–1928); Edmund A. Howe (1928–1930); Truman J. Lathrop (1930); Eugene Coleman (1930–1943)

Circa 1880s view. (National Archives)

U.S. Coast Guard

Charles Gardner (relief keeper, ca. 1940); Warren Alley (1943–?); Oscar M. "Tiny" Sparrow (ca. 1940s); Wilbur Brewster (1948–1951); Irving T. Sparrow (1951–1953); Robert McWilliams (ca. 1954–1955); Bruce Reed (ca. 1957–1959); Boyd L. Davis (ca. 1950s); John Johnson (ca. 1961); Leo R. Midgett (ca. 1964); Allan E. Wilson (ca. 1960s); Alfred Paul Chadwick (Coast Guard, ca. 1967); David K. Winchester (ca. 1967–1968); Arnold P. Chadwick (ca. late 1960s); Michael Carbino (ca. 1971–1973); Michael Hackett (1973–1975); Richard Harrison (1975–1977); Ronald O'Brien (1977–1979); John Terry (1979–1984); Robert French (1984–1986); Russell Ahlgren (1986–1987)

Nathaniel Otterson

(1879–1885)

Nathaniel Otterson was born in Hooksett, New Hampshire, in 1826. He and his wife, Judith Ann (Johnson) Otterson, had a son, John, and a daughter, Mary Jane.

Otterson made the pages of a newspaper called the *Mirror and Farmer* on May 1, 1875. According to the brief story, Otterson tracked two raccoons through the woods for two miles and cornered them in a hollow tree. He cut the tree down and bagged his game, according to the newspaper. Otterson sent half of one of the raccoons to his cousin, General Nathaniel "Natt" Head. The animals were "remarkably fat and made rich dinners," according to the *Mirror and Farmer.*

Otterson had no experience as a lighthouse keeper, and it isn't clear whether he had any sort of maritime experience. He was, however, the cousin of Natt Head, who began a term as governor of New Hampshire on June 5, 1879—less than a month before the lighthouse at the Nubble went into service.

It was the belief of historian Clifford Shattuck that Governor Head's influence with the customs collector in Portsmouth led to Otterson's appointment. Otterson's gift of raccoon meat to Head a few years earlier might have helped "grease the skids."

It appears that Otterson tried to take advantage of the lighthouse's status as a tourist draw, as some later keepers also did. An item in the August 7, 1880, issue of the *Portsmouth* (NH) *Journal* announced, "Visitors are not allowed to visit the lighthouse at York Nubble between the hours of 6 P.M. and 10 A.M.; but at other times the son of the keeper will row you over and back in his boat for ten cents."

When Otterson resigned following six years at the Nubble, a local newspaper reported that his leaving was "much to everyone's regret." Nathaniel Otterson lived out his years in his hometown of Hooksett. He died in 1891 and is buried at the Head Cemetery.

Circa 1890s view. (from the collection of the author)

Brackett Lewis
(1885–1904)

Brackett Lewis, who was born at Kittery Point, Maine, in 1848, was the longest serving keeper in the history of Cape Neddick Light Station. After enlisting at the age of 15, he saw action in the Maine infantry during the Civil War in 1864–1865. After being held as a prisoner in Virginia for a time, he mustered out of the military in July 1865.

Lewis had one daughter, Hattie, with his first wife, Addy. He later had another daughter, Annette, with his second wife, Sybil. He had two years of experience as an assistant keeper at Whaleback Lighthouse in Kittery before being appointed to the Nubble in September 1885.

Lewis continued the practice of rowing visitors to the island for ten cents per round-trip. Among the visitors spotted fishing from the island

Early 1900s postcard image. The man rowing the dory is probably Keeper Brackett Lewis.
(from the collection of the author)

in June 1899 was Senator William E. Mason of Illinois.

In August 1889, it was reported in a local newspaper that a visitor, while fishing on the Nubble, slipped and fell, causing his shoulder to become dislocated. Lewis rowed the unfortunate man from the island through the surf to Long Sands Beach. From there, he was taken to Portsmouth where, after treatment, he was "considerably shaken up, but merry as ever."

There was another incident in October 1892, when a Mr. W. K. Barrett, a pharmacy clerk at York Beach, accidentally shot himself in the leg while duck hunting on the rocks across from the Nubble. Lewis heard the man's cries from the lighthouse, according to a newspaper account. Lewis rowed across the channel and arranged for the man to be transported to a doctor, where he was reported to be "doing as well as could be expected."

Fog was a constant bane of a Maine lighthouse keeper's existence, and July was often one of the foggiest months. In July 1898, a newspaper report announced that the fog bell at the Nubble had been sounding during at least part of every day for a month, with the exception of two days. Lewis claimed he was so accustomed to the sound of the bell that he no longer noticed it, and he sometimes forgot to stop the bell after the fog had disappeared.

The newspaper also reported that Lewis had been ordered to no longer transport visitors to the island on Sundays. He had been earning about $12 each Sunday by providing boat transportation. Lewis complained that government officials felt he was making too much money, but the real reason was probably that it was suspected that the constant flow of tourists distracted his attention from his duties.

Interviewed late in his stay, Lewis said he had seen storms when the spray reached the top of the lighthouse. It was difficult, he said, to keep the lantern glass clean in winter. Lewis said that the visitors kept him busy going back and forth in summer, but the winters could get lonely.

The Lewis's daughter Annette married George Terry, a motorman on the Portsmouth, Kittery, and York trolley line, in the keeper's house on December 20, 1899. Also during the family's

stay, the keeper's daughter Hattie married Charles Billings of Kittery in the lighthouse lantern room.

Circa 1905. (from the Library of Congress)

After his retirement from lighthouse keeping, Brackett Lewis lived in Kittery for the remainder of his life. When he died in July 1931, it was noted that he had been last seen in public when he rode as a Civil War veteran in Kittery's Fourth of July parade that year. According to his obituary, he "was a man of genial disposition and kindly nature and had a host of friends." His grave is in Kittery's First Baptist Church Cemetery.

Circa 1905 postcard view.
(from the collection of the author)

William M. Brooks
(1904–1912)

William Brooks was born in Kittery, Maine, in 1863. He had previously served four years as an assistant keeper at remote Boon Island Light, followed by seven years at White Island Light in the Isles of Shoals. Brooks married Hanna M. Knight in 1886. He and his wife had one son, Henry, who was 17 when the family moved to the Nubble in December 1904. Henry lived with an aunt in Portsmouth when school was in session and spent vacations at the light station.

The *Portsmouth Herald* reported in July 1906 that Brooks had "many times been of assistance to distressed small craft near his light and deserved much praise for his ever ready aid." Once, while Brooks was checking the light at midnight, he became aware of a boater who was honking a horn to attract attention. Brooks went out in his dory and found that the vessel was filling with water, and he helped get it safely to shore. He once complained to a newspaper reporter that while there were four lifesaving stations on the New Hampshire coast, there were none in the long stretch between Portsmouth and Biddeford, Maine.

Henry Brooks died of rheumatic fever in September 1908 at the age of 21. His was the first of several deaths of keepers' family members that some have attributed to a curse.

William and Hanna Brooks were profiled in an article in the *Sanford Tribune* in August 1911. They were "most affable" and never grew weary of the "same old questions" being asked about the lighthouse. After their years at isolated light stations at Boon Island and White Island, they liked the Nubble best because of its closeness to the mainland. Brooks maintained a tiny garden patch on the island, growing beans and potatoes. The article continued:

Mrs. Brooks still delights in showing her visitors about and explaining how two small brass lamps of parlor-table size suffice for the lighthouse warning because the glass through which they shine magnifies

(photo by the author)

and refracts through prisms so as to concentrate all the rays. . . . All in all, according to Mr. and Mrs. Brooks, lighthouse service at The Nubble is rather delightful, at least to people of their temperament.

Like his predecessors, Brooks offered tourists a round-trip boat ride to the island for ten cents. He took it a step further, however, by placing a signboard across from the island, indicating that there was a ferry, fare 10¢. Rose Cushing Labrie, author of *Sentinel of the Sea: Nubble Light*, interviewed Brooks when he was in his 90s. He recalled his ferry service to the island, and he said that an additional five cents was charged for a tour of the station, led by his wife.

Timmie the Cat.
(from the collection of the author)

William and Hanna Brooks had a pet cat named Timmie when they moved from White Island to the Nubble. Six years later, Timmie was featured in a story in the *Boston Post*. He was said to be very handsome and to be much admired by the throngs of tourists who visited the Nubble in summer. Hanna Brooks claimed, "Few cats are more knowing or more compassionate."

Timmie was again featured in an article in the *Sanford Tribune* in 1911. He was 14 years old by that time and was described as "old tar, a first-rate sailor" who for many years was the "daily companion of Mr. Brooks on his fishing trips." Timmie had by that time retired to spending much time out in sunny nooks among the island's rocks, and by the hearth fire in the keeper's house.

Lighthouse Service officials took note that there were as many as 200 to 300 people on the island on busy summer days and that visitors were encouraged to fish with the use of equipment furnished by the keeper. Brooks resigned as keeper by late 1912. It seems likely that he was ordered to end the ferry service, and he may have felt that the loss of income made it impossible to remain as keeper.

After his lighthouse years, Brooks ran the Bay View Hotel in York for a time, and he also worked at the Portsmouth Naval Shipyard. When he died in December 1959 at the age of 95, it was reported that he had been the oldest retired employee of the shipyard. His grave is in the First Congregational Church Cemetery on Pepperrell Road in Kittery.

Circa 1910. (Library of Congress)

William Brooks in later years.
(photo by Rose Labrie)

James M. Burke
(1912–1919)

After about a quarter century at the offshore stations on Boon Island and Burnt Island, Maine, and White Island, New Hampshire, James Monroe Burke became keeper at the Nubble in 1912. Burke was born in Portsmouth, New Hampshire, in 1848.

Representing the fourth generation of seafaring men in his family, Burke went to sea on fishing boats and coastal trading vessels at the age of 14, and he eventually captained fishing vessels before turning to lighthouse keeping in 1888, when he was appointed second assistant keeper at Boon Island. While at that remote station, Burke was credited with rescuing the crew of a disabled schooner in a gale.

James Burke after his lighthouse-keeping days. (courtesy of William O. Thomson)

Burke arrived at the Nubble with his second wife, Addie (Orne) of Boothbay, Maine. He had two sons and a daughter from a first marriage. One of his sons, Charles, was keeper at Wood Island Light, not many miles up the coast off Biddeford Pool, Maine. James and Addie Burke had one daughter, Lucy. A newspaper report on the family's arrival in 1912 stated that Addie and Lucy would live on the mainland to make it easier for the girl to attend school.

Addie Burke died in March 1914 "after a lingering illness," and the government provided a lighthouse tender to transport the family to Boothbay Harbor for the funeral.

An article in the *Boston Herald* in January 1915 stated that Burke deserved to be on that year's "hero list." He towed a disabled launch to the light station on one occasion and cared for the occupants overnight, and on another day he rescued a man named Samuel L. Lewis, "whom he took from the water, provided with dry clothes, and cared for." Lewis, who had been fishing when a wave knocked him into the ocean, later said he owed his life to James Burke.

In a letter to author Clifford Shattuck in the late 1970s, James Burke's daughter Lucy Glidden Burke Steffen later recalled other details of life on the Nubble:

We all had lots of work to do, as everything had to be immaculate throughout the house as well as the lighthouse tower. In fact, cleanliness had to prevail throughout all the buildings as we had to pass inspection each month.

The government ship brought out supplies twice a year; for instance, oil, which was stored in the red brick building. My father was allowed just so many "rations." I really cannot remember the amounts, but I do recall getting our coal; and we received 100 lb. bags of beans, also sugar, flour, and molasses in large quantities.

We had lots of company, weather permitting. Many of my schoolmates used to enjoy coming over to the Nubble, some just to spend the day, some to spend the night or possibly to stay for a few days. Sometimes the sea got rough and they HAD to stay. We had an organ in the living room, which I used to play, and we all had such

good times singing the old songs.

Our home was a very comfortable six-room house, having a very pleasant living room, a nice size dining room, a large kitchen with pantry, and three bedrooms upstairs. But, of course, no bathroom.

We had a large parlor stove, which seemed to heat most of the house very well. Even though a severe storm might be blowing up outside, we were nice and cozy.

Burke used a section of the dining room to work on his records and reports. According to Lucy, so much detail was required for the monthly reports that it took her father three days to compile them.

Circa 1920 postcard view.
(from the collection of the author)

11:—NUBBLE LIGHT AT NIGHT, YORK BEACH, MAINE

42817

Nubble Light House, York Me.

were here tr. would *This is where I was last night* with you

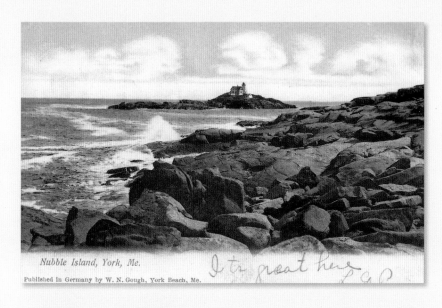

Nubble Island, York, Me.

Published in Germany by W. N. Gough, York Beach, Me.

I ts great here L G P

ON THE ROAD TO THE NUBBLE. YORK BEACH. ME.

(from the collection of the author)

A submarine telephone line was extended from the Nubble to the Boon Island Light Station about six miles away in 1917. Lucy made the first call to the keepers at Boon Island on May 31, 1917.

During World War I, military personnel joined the Burkes on the Nubble, where they kept watch for enemy submarines. The light was dimmed on some nights and extinguished on others, the intention being to confuse "possible submersibles."

Like many lighthouse families, the Burkes kept a cow and chickens on the island. Burke went duck hunting and fishing to supplement his family's food supply. Lobsters, crabs, periwinkles, and mussels were also plentiful near the island. The best fishing was about three or four miles from the Nubble, halfway to Boon Island, where Burke often caught large cod, haddock, and cusk. Some of the fish were dried and salted and later used to make fish cakes or creamed codfish.

During extreme low tides, it was sometimes possible to walk across the channel to the mainland. Lucy recalled being carried piggyback across the bar by her father, who would wear hip boots for the occasion. She also recalled the large numbers of birds that would fly into the tower at night; the family sometimes had to rake up hundreds of them that lay dead on the ground in the morning.

After he retired at the end of March 1919, Burke opened a small fish, bait, and grocery shop just down the street from the Nubble, at the corner of Broadway and Fort Hill Avenue. For some years, Burke spent his summers in York and winters at his home with his third wife, Fannie, in Wolfeboro, New Hampshire. Burke died in 1935 and is buried at the Lakeview Cemetery in Wolfeboro.

CAPTAIN BURKE'S STORE

A small store at 104 Broadway in York was opened by retired Nubble light keeper James Burke in the 1920s. Burke ran the store each summer, selling bamboo fishing poles, bait, ice cream, and cold drinks; the store also seems to have functioned as a real estate office. Charles E. King later purchased the property from Burke and continued to operate the store.

Rachel Carpenter purchased the building in the late 1950s. It's no longer operated as a store, but the Carpenter family still lovingly maintains the little building. It's marked with a sign: Capt. Burke's Store, Circa 1920.

Postcard view of Captain Burke's Store. (courtesy of Herb Carpenter)

Captain Burke's Store as it looks today. (photo by the author)

William P. Richardson
(1919–1921)

William Richardson, the next keeper, had a short two-year stay. He had been an assistant keeper at the "Two Lights" in Cape Elizabeth, Maine, where he nearly drowned in October 1911. He had been fishing in one of the station's boats when it was flipped by a wave. As Richardson struggled to swim for shore, he was rescued by the crew at the nearby lifesaving station.

During his relatively brief stay at the Nubble, Richardson's son died of croup; he was the third successive keeper to lose a family member to illness. The days of the "Nubble ferry" seem to have come to an end with Richardson, who was discharged for ferrying visitors for a fee. He returned to his home in Portland, Maine.

Fairfield H. Moore
(1921–1928)

Fairfield Moore—a Maine native born in 1871—had been an assistant keeper at Maine's Whitehead Light for several years and principal keeper at Rockland Breakwater Light for four years before he came to the Nubble. Moore and his wife, Helen (Dolliver), had four children, and two grandchildren were born on the island during Moore's stay. They were the first children born in the keeper's house.

Phyllis Moore Searles, the keeper's daughter, gave birth to a baby girl named Helen on August 23, 1923. Then, in March 1927, Moore's daughter Eva and her husband James Kimball welcomed another baby girl, Barbara. According to the historian William O. Thomson, there was sleet and snow along with high winds on the day Barbara was born, but Keeper Moore rowed through the storm to fetch the doctor from the mainland; the doctor and Moore arrived back at the island just moments before the baby's arrival. According to Thomson, Grandma Helen had been a "true midwife."

Two more children were later born on the island to Eva and James Kimball. Their son, James—the first boy

Fairfield Moore.
(courtesy of Barbara Finnemore)

born on the Nubble—died as a small child after the family had left the station, adding fuel to the talk of a curse on Nubble keepers and their families.

Moore's granddaughter Barbara Kimball Finnemore, who lived on the island until she was six, later shared some memories with William O. Thomson. When she started attending school, her grandfather rowed her across the channel every morning, and a local man picked her up and drove

her to school. Barbara's companion on the island was an all-black mutt named Karzen, who enjoyed playing hide and seek with the girl. One of her favorite memories was ascending the lighthouse stairs and watching her grandfather "light up" for the night.

On July 24, 1926, a violent storm knocked the fog bell tower off its foundation and moved it about four feet. Moore would normally have sounded the bell during the storm, but he didn't dare because the tower was precariously close to the edge of the bluff, and he feared it might plunge into the sea if the striking machinery was activated. Repairs were swiftly completed.

Moore made the *Portsmouth Herald* in August 1928, when a school of large fish—12 to 18 feet in length—was observed close to the Nubble. Moore theorized that the fish were sturgeon, but others believed them to be tuna. Either would have been rare in the vicinity.

Moore returned to Rockland Breakwater Light in 1928. He spent six more years as keeper there and died suddenly in April 1934. He is buried in the First Parish Cemetery in York Village.

Barbara Finnemore, who was born on the Nubble in 1927, gathered with her grandchildren for her 90th birthday in March 2017. (photo by Debbie Jones)

Edmund A. Howe

(1928–1930)

We know little about Edmund Howe's brief stay at the Nubble, which lasted just a little over a year. He had been keeper at Great Duck Island Light in Maine's Acadia region for eight years before coming to the Nubble on October 31, 1928.

Howe's first wife had died in 1921, and the most notable event during his tenure at the Nubble was his marriage to his former housekeeper, Emily Williams. The ceremony took place in the living room of the keeper's house with a local Baptist minister officiating. Williams had been Howe's housekeeper for several years at Great Duck Island before his transfer to the Nubble.

(photo by the author)

(photo by the author)

In November 1928, Howe wrote to his superiors in the Lighthouse Service and asked, "Am I supposed to go ashore after everyone that comes down to the bank and calls me? If I do, I shan't get much chance to do anything else." He was told that providing transportation to visitors was not a priority and that two previous keepers had in fact been dismissed for devoting too much attention to the "Nubble ferry."

Howe's health deteriorated, and he resigned and entered the Marine Hospital in February 1930. Truman Lathrop served as the temporary keeper for 15 days on Howe's departure. Howe died in June 1932 at the age of 69 and is buried in the Oak Hill Cemetery in Winterport, Maine.

Eugene L. Coleman
(1930–1943)

Eugene Leslie Coleman, born in Georgetown, Maine, in 1888, sailed on schooners from Georgetown and Bath for about a decade before becoming a lighthouse keeper. He spent a brief time as an assistant at the Fort Popham Light Station and then about seven years as an assistant keeper at remote Boon Island before winning an assignment to the Nubble. Coleman married Amanda (Varner) in 1919; they had no children, but they did have a companion who became quite famous: a cat named Sambo Tonkus.

Eugene and Amanda Coleman.
(from the collection of Bob Trapani, Jr.)

SAMBO TONKUS

Sambo Tonkus, also known as "Mr. T.," was a burly tabby cat first brought to the Nubble by Keeper James Burke. He was transported to the island when he was two weeks old, "in a doughnut box with a coot's leg," according to a newspaper story. He was passed from keeper to keeper and was pretty far along in cat years by the time Eugene and Amanda Coleman arrived in 1930.

Sambo Tonkus earned widespread fame because of his penchant for crossing the channel between the Nubble and the mainland three or four times day. He was a proficient mouser, and with the eradication of mice on the island, he would search for prey among the rocks on the mainland.

In August 1935, the *Biddeford Daily Journal* reported: "The life evidently agrees with Sambo, for he weighs over 19 pounds today at the age of almost 12 years and strolls nonchalantly about seaweed-covered rocks looking for anything of interest which may turn up in the intervals of his lighthouse duties. . . . He is perfectly willing to pose for a picture with visitors, even children, as well as with his master."

The big cat became a celebrity to regular visitors, who would watch and wait for him to make his trips across the channel. His swimming must have come as quite a surprise to those tourists who hadn't heard about him in advance.

Sambo Tonkus.
(from the collection of Bob Trapani, Jr.)

A personnel document from early in Coleman's stay indicates that his yearly gross pay was $1,740 and that he was "subject to duty at all hours while on station." In 1930, the year of his arrival, Coleman recorded over 1,000 visitors in his guest register, including guests from 11 nations and 32 states. The register showed totals of from 722 to 1,092 visitors yearly between 1930 and 1934.

The popular and prolific New England maritime historian Edward Rowe Snow visited with Eugene and Amanda Coleman in August 1941. Amanda, an expert at crocheting, showed Snow some beautiful pieces she had created. Snow and Eugene Coleman went to the top of the tower and looked toward Bald Head Cliff, scene of the *Isidore* tragedy in 1842. "It's a hopeless place to be in," said Coleman, "and many is the fine ship or schooner which has met her fate on the jagged ledges over there."

Coleman told Snow about a time when he was crossing to the island in the station's dory with his wife, a friend, and some groceries. The dory capsized, but everyone made it to shore safely. There were, according to Snow, some "minor injuries to the groceries."

Eugene Coleman and Sambo Tonkus. (courtesy of William O. Thomson)

During the Colemans' stay, the first indoor toilet was installed along with a saltwater septic system. Electricity came to the island in 1938. During World War II, the light was extinguished, and a lookout tower was built on the island. A contingent of Coast Guardsmen kept a 24-hour eye out for German U-boats.

The Colemans were pleased with a transfer to Cape Cod's Nauset Light in 1943, after 12 years and eight months at the Nubble. Coleman told Edward Rowe Snow, "Everything we wanted at the other two lighthouses had to be brought out from shore. . . . It is indeed a comfortable feeling to know that we can get our groceries without using a boat."

Eugene Coleman, widely known as "Colie," retired from his 32-year light-keeping career in 1955. When they retired, Amanda said she liked their last station, Bass Harbor Head Light, best of all because of its easy accessibility. At Bass Harbor, she was even able to participate in a garden club. Eugene Coleman died in February 1966 and is buried at the Oak Grove Cemetery in Bath, Maine.

Circa 1950 postcard view.
(from the collection of the author)

The Coast Guard Years, 1943–1987

The U.S. Coast Guard took over the management of the nation's lighthouses from the old civilian Lighthouse Service in 1939. When Eugene Coleman left the Nubble in 1943, he was followed by a succession of Coast Guard keepers. Information on many of the Coast Guard keepers is sparse, but here is what we know about some of them.

Warren A. Alley (1943–?)

Warren Austin Alley, who was born in Jonesport, Maine, in 1896, was a veteran of World War I. He became the Coast Guard's keeper at the Nubble after a few years at two rugged offshore stations, Whaleback and Boon Island. Alley was married to Mary Elizabeth (Davis), who was also from Jonesport.

Alley's grandson, Warren Day, lived at the Nubble for about a year and

(photo by the author)

a half. In a 2003 interview, he mentioned that the family had three goats, a dog, and two cats on the island. Day recalled that trips to the mainland were made in a 12-foot skiff, and the family also had a 16-foot boat with an outboard motor. Alley's wife sometimes went for months at a time without going ashore. When they left the Nubble, transportation on the mainland was a 1936 Studebaker.

Warren Day and his grandfather kept about 24 lobster traps around the Nubble, and Day sold his catch to a lobster pound at Long Sands Beach for 35 cents a pound. Day also often fished from the skiff, catching small fish to be used as bait in the traps and larger fish for the dinner table.

The USO sent boxes of books and magazines to the Nubble, including the *Saturday Evening Post*, so there was always plenty to read. Day helped his grandfather with the care of the lighting apparatus, and he helped with tours for visitors. He also built lobster traps. When he had spare time, his favorite pastime was sitting on the rocks and daydreaming.

Once, late at night, Warren Day and his grandfather heard some noise out on the water. They went out in the skiff and discovered a schooner that was in trouble in rough seas. "They were out there drinking and dragging anchor," he said later. The Coast Guard and the fire department were called, and the people aboard the schooner were safely rescued.

Day said that his time at lighthouses with his grandparents "could never have been more wonderful. It was an anchor for me." Warren Alley died in 1962 and is buried at the Greenwood Cemetery in Jonesport, Maine.

Wilbur I. Brewster
(1948–1951)

Wilbur "Bill" Brewster, who came to the Nubble after some years at White Island Light in the Isles of Shoals, was profiled by Leon F. Jackson in the March 1951 issue of a magazine called *Shoreliner*. A bachelor, Brewster lived with his "ever faithful companion"—a bloodhound named Brutus—along with a parrot and lovebirds. Accord-

Wilbur Brewster and his dog, Brutus, circa 1950.
(collection of the author)

Wilbur Brewster coming ashore
for mail and groceries, circa 1950.
(collection of the author)

ing to the article, Brewster also made friends with many wild birds and tried to protect them from the hawks and owls that sometimes visited the island.

Brewster loved fishing, and Jackson wrote that a fishing trip with him was "a never-to-be-forgotten experience." Brewster knew the best fishing spots around the area and the precise times when the fishing would be optimal. Bill Brewster retired from the Coast Guard later in 1951 after 26 years of service.

Elson L. Small

(substitute keeper, ca. 1948)

Elson Leroy Small, a Maine native who had a 28-year career as a lighthouse keeper in the Lighthouse Service and Coast Guard, was the keeper from 1946 to 1948 a few miles down the coast at Portsmouth Harbor Lighthouse. A few times, Small and his wife, Connie, filled in at the Nubble when Wilbur Brewster went on vacation.

Elson Small at the Nubble, 1940s. (courtesy of the American Lighthouse Foundation)

Connie later wrote in her book *The Lighthouse Keeper's Wife* that she "felt like a goldfish in a bowl" because of all the tourists who were always looking at the lighthouse and its residents.

Elson and Connie Small outside the keeper's house at Portsmouth Harbor Light Station in the 1940s. (courtesy of Connie Small)

Connie wrote that Brewster's pet parrot loved to chatter to her husband's banjo playing. If Elson stopped playing and started for the door, the parrot would say, "Come back here!" The bird also learned to say, "I'd like coffee, Connie."

Connie and Elson tried to keep Brewster's dog, Brutus, harnessed outside, but he continually wiggled out of his harness and came back into the house—a problem for Connie, who was allergic to dogs.

Elson Small died in 1960. Connie Small, one of the most beloved figures of the New England lighthouse community, died at 103 in 2005.

Irving T. Sparrow
(1951–1953)

Irving Thompson Sparrow, a native of Maryland, spent many years as a Coast Guard light keeper along the New England coast in the 1940s and 1950s with his wife, Gloria, and their two children, Orelia and Irving, Jr.

Besides his years at the Nubble, Sparrow was keeper of the lighthouses at Perkins Island, Ram Island Ledge, and Seguin Island in Maine, and at Eastern Point in Gloucester, Massachusetts.

Orelia Sparrow, seven years old at the time, made the *Portsmouth Herald* in March 1952. The newspaper reported that her father rowed Orelia to shore each seasonable morning to go to school at York Beach. The keeper then met his daughter on the mainland every afternoon to row her back home.

After Sparrow's retirement, he and his wife lived in Virginia Beach and later on Maryland's Eastern Shore.

1950s postcard.
(from the collection of the author)

Bruce C. Reed
(1956–1959)

Bruce Reed moved to the Nubble with his wife, Marjorie, and their two young children, Steven and Lynne, in 1956 after two years at Maine's Pond Island Light Station. At their new station, the Reeds had many conveniences that were lacking at remote Pond Island, including indoor plumbing, electricity, and even television.

In a 1987 letter, Reed provided some details of life on the Nubble in the 1950s:

> There was a hand winch in the boathouse, which I soon had replaced with an electric one. The furnace was coal operated at that time, and I had that replaced with fuel oil and a diesel generator in the fuel shed (the red building). There were also about 30 steps to the top of the rock, then a mud path from there to the porch. I requisitioned lumber to extend the steps and built a walkway to the porch.

NUBBLE LIGHT
YORK, ME.

Nubble Light, York, Me.

No. 71   Moore & Gibson Co. N. Y.   Germany

NUBBLE LIGHT, YORK BEACH, ME.

NUBBLE LIGHT, YORK BEACH, MAINE

(from the collection of the author)

Marge worked in the gift shop on the point across from the island during the summer months. I think the buildings on the point have changed a lot since we were there. The gift shop was on the left side of the point, as you look out from the front of the lighthouse, and across from it on the right side was a lobster pound and restaurant.

I had a lobster license and was able to catch quite a few lobsters for ourselves and some for relatives. We also got quite a lot of fish and crabs. Since then, we've often reflected on how fortunate we were then to dine on such expensive fare.

One year while we were there, we had relatives visiting on the 4th of July weekend. We stacked all the driftwood we could find down on the lower end of the island and then built a frame of a house and door, etc. in front of the pile. We then set a timer to burn it for a 4th of July bonfire. It made a big hit with those people who were parked on the point that night.

When I got bored, I occasionally would go out in the light tower, sit on the steps, and play my harmonica. The acoustics were fantastic!

Bruce Reed and family. (U.S. Coast Guard photo)

Steven Reed, who was five years old when the family left the island, said that almost 60 years later, when walking on any stairs, his mind still flashed to trips up and down the stairs to the boathouse at the Nubble. He shared additional memories in 2017 correspondence:

Sometimes when the supply ship came, my dad would lock my sister and me in the upstairs bedroom. I assume it would be at those times when my mom was working in a little gift shop on the mainland. One time my sister and I had the brilliant idea to throw all our clothes, including what we were wearing, out the upstairs window onto the front lawn. When my dad was done with the supply ship, he came and let us out so we could go down and pick up our clothes, naked of course.

There was a pile of rope under my bed, and I used to think of it as snakes. Later in life, I learned it was actually a rope ladder to be used for escape in case of fire.

The only other thing I remember was that a cat we had came out from under the house with all kinds of dust all over its face, and I thought for sure it was some kind of monster preparing to eat me.

The Reeds were surprised to find that tourists frequently walked across to the island at low tide. A relative, Abby Saffold, later wrote that it was "disconcerting to be working in the kitchen and look up to see the faces of

Steve Reed with a prize catch in the kitchen of the keeper's house, 1959. (courtesy of Steve Reed)

eager tourists pressed against the windows." Sometimes, the tourists would be stuck on the island when the tide rose, and Reed would ferry them back to the mainland.

Abby Saffold also wrote that the cleanliness of the station during the Reeds' stay made a big impression on her. "Fresh paint everywhere and no dust and dirt," she wrote.

In 1959, Bruce Reed installed the original version of the trolley system that was used to transport supplies to

Circa 1950s. (U.S. Coast Guard photo)

Bruce Reed cleaning the Fresnel lens at Nubble Light. (courtesy of Steve Reed)

and from the island—a simple wooden box suspended from a cable, sent back and forth with a hand-over-hand manual pulley system. Steven sat in the box for a photo, but he never rode it across the channel. The trolley system was employed to help get the family's belongings off the island when they left in 1959.

Bruce Reed later wrote, "We were sad to finally leave the lighthouse, but when our son got to school age, the Coast Guard wouldn't allow us to stay with a child being transported every day. They later changed the rule, but it was too late for us." After his Coast Guard service, Bruce Reed moved to southern California. He died in Huntington, California, in March 2013.

(courtesy of Steve Reed)

July 1958.

Seas breaking over the rocks in November 1958.

Bruce Reed working at the Nubble in July 1958.

Lynne Reed at the base of the lighthouse, October 1958.

A view from the top of the lighthouse in July 1958.

A Coast Guard boat at the ramp in July 1958.

An August 1957 boat ride to Boon Island Light Station.

Marjorie Reed in the kitchen, September 1957.

Lynne and Steve Reed at the base of the lighthouse

Lynne Reed with cousin Ricky in the keeper's house in November 1957.

Marjorie and Bruce Reed in the keeper's house, February 1958.

A view in February 1958. Notice the helicopter across from the island.

The steps to the boathouse, 1957.

In the keeper's house in February 1958: Steve and Lynne Reed with Gram Bea. Notice the kids' red dinette set in the kitchen.

Steve and Lynne Reed on the porch of the keeper's house in 1957.

Heavy seas at the boat ramp in November 1957.

Lynne and Steve Reed in the "yard" at the Nubble, September 1957.

Steve and Lynne Reed inside the lighthouse, September 1958.

Bruce Creswell
(ca. 1959–1960)

Aerial view circa 1960. (U.S. Coast Guard photo)

John Johnson
(ca. 1961–1962)

Bruce Creswell and his wife, Shirley, came to the Nubble in early 1959. For years, the newspaper *Maine Coast Fisherman* had a regular "Lighthouse Page," with letters from lighthouse keepers from around New England. In November 1960, Caswell wrote the following in a letter to the *Maine Coast Fisherman*:

Here comes that time of year again, the time you start working on the inside. But stop—I haven't finished the outside yet! Last year my wife Shirley and I painted all the outside of the buildings and got the station looking good and during the winter worked on the inside. This summer we spot-painted the outside again, but after [Hurricane] Donna went through, we had to start all over again because the wind and rain just pushed its way through.

In early 1962, John Johnson, Coast Guard keeper at the Nubble, wrote to the *Maine Coast Fisherman*: "We had a good winter here, although as it is my wife's first try at lighthouse keeping, she had to adjust from being away from home. We both come from Bath, Maine. Winter passed quite fast, as we were busy painting most of the time. Now the outside season is just about here."

David Winchester
(1966–1968)

Twenty-six-year-old David Winchester arrived as the Coast Guard keeper in 1966, along with his wife, Patricia Jaye—known as "P. Jaye"—and their children Robyn and Rick. In November 1966, Winchester took his pregnant wife to the mainland where she caught a Greyhound bus to Portland, Maine. Their third child, Wendianne, was born the next day.

David Winchester at the Nubble. (courtesy of Richard Winchester)

David once broke his big toe and couldn't climb the lighthouse stairs for a time, so P. Jaye filled in and tended the light. The TV got only three channels, but there was plenty to do. The children explored the island and drew pictures, and the whole family did lots of reading. "It was just a utopia, a wonderful place for the children," said P. Jaye in a 2009 interview. She later described the family's time at the Nubble as the "best time" of her life. "Never a moment were we bored," she said.

The trolley system, with a basket suspended from a cable from the mainland to the island, first installed in the late 1950s, was not intended for the transportation of people; it was intended for the transport of supplies. The Winchesters used it creatively. When they returned to the island after Wendianne was born, P. Jaye and her baby went across in the basket.

"It wasn't that big a deal," she recalled later, in an article on Seacoastonline. com. "We were so used to it. [David] took the suitcases and all the baby formula and went to the island [in the boat]. There was no baby life jacket

Rick Winchester in the basket in 1967. (collection of the author)

THE BOY IN THE BASKET

The Nubble's trolley system, a basket suspended on a cable that stretched across the channel between the island and the mainland, was intended to move supplies, not people. Over the years, some people had other ideas about it. In 1967, the Coast Guard light keeper David Winchester and his wife, P. Jaye, got into the habit of putting their young son, Rick, in the basket each morning to send him on his way to the second grade at a nearby school.

P. Jaye Winchester later said that she thought the basket was safer than traveling across in a boat. "There were a lot of mornings Rick would not have been able to go to school in that boat because of the swell. You needed to bring the boat in at a slant. You had to count the waves to get up on those rocks. Otherwise, you would have been swamped. I felt very safe [in the basket]," she said. In a recent interview, Rick said he was "never scared" and enjoyed the "bucket rides."

A photographer snapped a picture of Rick in the basket, and the photo was picked up by the Associated Press and appeared widely in newspapers—even in the Southeast Asia edition of the U.S. Army newspaper, *Stars and Stripes*. The district commander saw the photo in a Boston paper and decided that riding in the basket was too dangerous for children.

Rick boarded with the family of a classmate on the mainland for a while after that, returning to his family on the weekends. The Winchesters' expected stint on the island was cut short by a few months when David was transferred to a mainland station. It became standard policy that families with school-age children were not sent to the Nubble.

A local artist, Madeline Downing, also painted a scene of the boy in the basket, and it won the York Harbor Art Show. The story later inspired a children's book, *Trouble at Nubble Light* by Katherine Bailey.

for Wendy. She and I climbed into the bucket. I'll never forget, two elderly ladies saw us. The gasps were deafening. I climbed in. I was just so anxious to get home. He pulled us over. He secured the box. Then we were home. I waved to the ladies, 'We're safe.' They waved back, God love 'em.''

The Winchesters also used the trolley system to transport groceries, a crib for their baby, and other furniture, and even a Christmas tree. Most famously, they used it to send their son, Rick, to school.

Sundays were a big day for the Winchester family, especially in the summer. After breakfast, they'd all get their swimsuits and goggles, and they'd play in the water near the boathouse. Young Robyn would be secured in a harness. The nice thing about the cove near the boathouse was that it was hidden from view from most of the tourists across on the mainland, affording some privacy for the family.

After some time stationed at the Coast Guard station at Woods Hole on Cape Cod, David Winchester served in the Vietnam War. David and P. Jaye

visited Nubble Light in 1997. "Some of my furniture was still there. The toilet still flushed saltwater," said P. Jaye. It was David's last visit; he died later in 1997.

Circa 1972 aerial view. (U.S. Coast Guard photo)

John Reidy
(relief keeper, 1965–1967)

While he was stationed at the Coast Guard station at Fletcher's Neck in Biddeford Pool, Maine, EN3 John Reidy was a Coast Guard relief keeper for three area lighthouses: Wood Island, Goat Island, and Cape Neddick. In a 2014 letter to the author, he wrote:

(photo by the author)

(photo by the author)

(photo by the author)

Getting supplies out to the Nubble was its own challenge. There was a peapod boat there, but it was seldom used because the ramp was not well sheltered. Further, there was not a dock on the mainland available close by. Instead, a cable car ran from the mainland out to the island. This car was little more than a wooden box, about five feet square. A cable was suspended on telephone poles that were installed at both ends and had platforms in place to load and unload whatever was needed.

When the extreme low tides of the moon occurred, it was possible to walk over the exposed rocks to get from the mainland to the island. This was not often possible and was dangerous when it was, due to the slippery seaweed. I recall one time when the refrigerator in the keeper's kitchen failed and required replacement. This equipment exchange was made via the cable car. Moving an upright refrigerator on a suspended cable car was certainly a very tense and frightening experience! Fortunately, this was done during the summer,

so hauling the new refrigerator from the cable car uphill to the lighthouse was accomplished with only the force of gravity to overcome. Also of note, movement of the cable car was done by hand over hand, not by means of any electric motors.

Circa 1972 aerial view, looking up the coast to the north. (U.S. Coast Guard photo)

Michael Carbino
(1971–1973)

Mike Carbino and his wife, Linda, were profiled in a 1972 article by Jim Martin in the *York County Coast Star*. Carbino was a first class boatswain's mate who had spent 10 years in the U.S. Navy, including a year and a half in Vietnam, where he captained a river supply boat.

The Carbinos lived on the Nubble with their young daughter, Mary. They often invited friends over in the evening, so they were rarely lonely— at least in the warmer months. Uninvited sightseers frequently crossed the channel to the island at low tide, and Carbino would tell them the island was closed. His main concern was the dangers of climbing on the island's slippery rocks.

Winters were another story. The Carbinos rarely left the island, and groceries were sent across using the basket on the cable. The colder months allowed plenty of time for Linda to do her knitting and sewing and for Mike to work on his hobby of making picture frames decorated with nautical braiding.

The telephone became their primary link to the mainland in the colder months. During one stretch of severe cold, a pipe that carried water from the cistern to the kitchen burst, leaving the Carbinos with no water. They called the York Beach Fire Department. A pumper truck soon arrived, and water was pumped across the channel to the keeper's house.

The Carbinos' daughter, Mary, three years old at the time of the 1972 article, was not allowed outside on her own. Her favorite activity was swimming in the little cove near the boathouse. Mike and Linda saw the Nubble as an ideal to place to raise a child, except that she had no other children as playmates.

During a severe nor'easter in February 1972, debris tossed by the waves broke one of the glass panes in the lantern. Carbino later said that during the storm, he looked out the window in his office in the keeper's house and found himself looking up at the waves, something he had never experienced. Linda said that the storm left the island coated with ice, looking like it was "covered with glass." Walkways were washed out, and the boathouse was knocked askew, leaving Carbino with plenty of repairs to complete. Lumber for the repairs was sent across to the island using the trolley system.

Mike and Linda Carbino said they were once told that the first place a couple goes after leaving a lighthouse is the divorce court. They laughed about that, and Mike said that light-

Along the Shore at Nubble Light, York Beach, Maine

Nubble Light at night, York Beach, Maine

Nubble Island Light, York Beach, Me.   4

Nubble Island, York Beach, Me.   Its alright for Friday

W. P. Fo.

Published in Germany by S. Dowallby.

(from the collection of the author)

Circa 1980s. (Historic American Buildings Survey, Library of Congress)

house duty was a pleasant change from some of his previous duty. Linda said, "We've gotten to know each other a lot better."

Michael Hackett

(1973–1974)

Mike Hackett and his wife, Sue, were both 23 years old when they were profiled in an article in the *Boston Globe* in March 1973, just a few weeks after they had moved to the Nubble. They had been married for three years,

and they had known each other since they attended high school together in Needham, Massachusetts. After some time spent aboard Coast Guard vessels, Hackett was pleased when he was assigned to the Nubble.

"We are not city types," said Sue. "We both love the seacoast, and so you can imagine how happy I was when Mike told me he got a transfer to a family lighthouse." She added that most of her daytime hours were spent indoors, cooking and cleaning and decorating. And she admitted to sometimes watching the daytime soap operas on TV that Mike thought were "stupid." Sue and Mike enjoyed going outside with a flashlight at night to "listen to the waves."

"If you are a party-type person, this would be the worst possible life to lead," Hackett told Warren H. Talbot, reporter for the *Globe*. "I mean, there's no bus stop at my front door to take me to a movie or to a pub. Our needs here are simple. All we need is a lot of blue jeans and sweaters and a lot of canned and frozen food. The work is hard but fun, but I'm telling you, we are rewarded with quiet nights, fresh air, and some of the most beautiful scenery in New England."

Historian Clifford Shattuck provided more details of the Hacketts' stint at the Nubble in his 1979 book on the light station. Sue's parents and sister helped the couple move to their new home, and a sudden storm left the whole party stranded on the island for almost three days. Food rations were nearly exhausted by the time calmer seas made an escape possible.

One time, the Hacketts called for a repairman to fix their Singer sewing machine. The repairman, who knew nothing about the place, waited for low tide, then walked across the channel and scaled the rocks to the lighthouse. The Hacketts were shocked when there was a knock on their door and they discovered the repairman, with his pants rolled up, shoes in one hand and toolkit in the other.

Boon Island Light, about six miles away, had multiple keepers, meaning someone there was always awake. It was one of the duties of the Coast Guard keepers at Boon Island to call the keeper at the Nubble if the foghorn was needed during the night. One night, as the Nubble disappeared in thick fog, no call came from Boon Island. A local lobsterman parked himself near the island and imitated the Nubble's sound signal with his own boat horn until Hackett finally woke up.

One of the more unusual calls the Hacketts received came at 2:00 a.m. from a man who asked, matter-of-factly, "How are surfing conditions near the station?"

Hackett told the *Boston Globe*, "This is the best possible duty in the Coast Guard." His biggest regret was that it was impossible to get Chinese food delivered to the lighthouse.

(photo by the author)

Richard Harrison
(1974–1977)

Dick Harrison and his wife, Sheila, moved to the Nubble in August 1974. A native of the area, Harrison had served four years in the U.S. Navy before he joined the Coast Guard. The kitchen was modernized around the time they arrived—a good thing for Harrison, who enjoyed cooking. Beef stew was a specialty.

A newspaper article in October 1974 described a typical day. Whoever got up first turned the light off in the lighthouse. Harrison raised the American flag, and then went to a tiny office on the second floor of the keeper's house to catch up on the station's daily records. Sheila most often did the weather reports, called in every four hours to the Coast Guard station in South Portland, Maine. The reports included sky conditions, visibility, wind direction and speed, height and frequency of waves, air temperature, and barometer reading. Sheila Harrison, an expert seamstress, filled some of her off hours by making clothing for her husband and herself. While Dick did most of the repairs, Sheila often helped with painting and lawn care. Dick Harrison escaped across to the mainland more often than his wife to get supplies, but Sheila said that friends and relatives often came to visit, and when there were no other people around, she still had her two dogs for company.

Ronald O'Brien
(1977–1979)

Ronald O'Brien—a native of Bennington, Vermont—was in charge at the Nubble during one of the worst storms in recorded New England history, the infamous blizzard of February 6–7, 1978. According to the historian William O. Thomson, O'Brien and his family had to take shelter in the lighthouse tower during the storm, as the house was being battered by rocks and other debris thrown by the waves. Rivers of foam washed right across the island, from the seaward side to the channel between the Nubble and the mainland. The storm destroyed the island's boathouse and walkways, and it was more than a week before the O'Briens were able to leave.

O'Brien's wife, Nancy, had a pet cat named Jack who would often wander across the channel to the mainland at low tide, when the crossing could be done across the rocks. He'd then find himself stranded when the tide came in. Unlike his famous predecessor, Sambo Tonkus, Jack wanted no part of swimming across the channel. Nancy would watch for Jack's green eyes peering over to the island, and she'd row across, toss him into a mail sack, and bring him back home. Nancy also had two German shepherds; one of them had a litter of five puppies on the island.

NUBBLE IN SPACE

Nubble is the only lighthouse to be sent into outer space—sort of. The *Voyager II* space probe was launched on August 20, 1977, to study the outermost planets in our solar system. The probe carried a gold-plated audio-visual disk that held scientific information, spoken greetings from people of Earth (including President Carter and the secretary general of the United Nations), music, sounds of whales and other sounds from Earth, along with various photographs of Earth, its life forms, and structures. Among the 116 photos encoded on the disk in analog form was a photo of the Nubble Lighthouse.

The material on the disk was intended for any intelligent extraterrestrial life form or for future humans who may find it. Whether an extraterrestrial life form would be capable of making sense out of a photo of a lighthouse is questionable, but as of late 2016, *Voyager II* was said to be one of the most distant human-made objects in existence, some 112.5 astronomical units from the sun.

The *Voyager II* spacecraft.
(NASA photo)

The gold record on *Voyager II*.
(NASA photo)

John Terry
(1979–1984)

Karyn and John Terry.
(courtesy of William O. Thomson)

John Terry spent five years as the Coast Guard keeper with his wife, Karyn, and two cats named Tuffy and Tiny. Elinor DeWire wrote about the cats in her book *The Lighthouse Menagerie: Stories of Animals at Lighthouses.* Tuffy and Tiny didn't swim to shore like a famous predecessor, but they enjoyed climbing the lighthouse stairs to the upper reaches, where there were always plenty of insects to catch. They also chased the island's plentiful gulls, but that pursuit never yielded any positive results.

Robert French
(1984–1986)

John Terry with Tuffy and Tiny in the lantern room. (courtesy of Elinor DeWire)

In his book *Nubble Light, York, Maine,* historian William O. Thomson wrote about Bob French and his wife, Kathie, who lived on the island from 1984 to 1986. During that time, a national TV commercial for Maxwell House coffee featured the Nubble Lighthouse. In the commercial, a stereotypical sea captain was seen drinking coffee at the lighthouse.

The Frenches told Thomson that

whenever they came ashore, everyone would ask them where the sea captain was. According to Thomson, they came up with some creative and fun answers to the question. Since he didn't pass them along, we'll just have to imagine what those answers were.

The Ahlgrens and the tramway basket circa 1986.
(U.S. Coast Guard photo)

Russell Ahlgren
(1986–1987)

Russ Ahlgren, the last Coast Guard keeper, lived on the island with his wife, Brenda, and their young son, Christopher, for about 18 months beginning in January 1986. Russ enjoyed fishing in his spare time, and he liked to snorkel in the cove near the boathouse. He once said that he was a "nervous wreck" during the brief periods when he left the island. "There's that chance that's something's going to happen. This is my job. I take it very seriously," he said.

One of the things the Ahlgrens enjoyed most was the helicopter visits of the "Flying Santa" at Christmastime. The tradition of Santa flying to bring gifts to people at lighthouses went back to 1929.

The Ahlgrens were sad to leave when the station was automated in July 1987. Russ told the *York Weekly* newspaper, "It's been an honor to be out here and to be part of the history of this light. We've got some real good friends in town that we're going to miss."

THE FLYING SANTA

William Wincapaw, a native of Friendship, Maine, was a pioneer in the early days of aviation. A skilled and adventurous pilot, he was most at home in amphibious airplanes. During many of his flights at night or in bad weather, lighthouses served as his primary means of navigation. He developed a deep appreciation for the dedication of keepers and their families. As a way of expressing his gratitude, on Christmas Day in 1929 he loaded his plane with newspapers, magazines, coffee, candy, and more, and he dropped packages at several lighthouses in midcoast Maine. The reaction was so positive that he expanded the flights in the years that followed, eventually reaching into other New England states. Wincapaw's son, Bill Jr., became a licensed pilot at the age of 16, and he took an active role in the flights.

Edward Rowe Snow, a schoolteacher in Winthrop, Massachusetts, who would become a popular historian and author, became involved in the Santa flights in the mid-1930s. For some years, Snow and Wincapaw shared Flying Santa duties. Snow's wife, Anna-Myrle, flew with her husband in 1940 and accompanied him each year after that. William Wincapaw died after apparently suffering a heart attack shortly after taking off from Rockland Harbor in July 1947, and Edward Rowe Snow continued as the sole Flying Santa, visiting 176 lighthouses from Canada to Florida in 1947. Since Snow was not a pilot, he hired a plane and pilot each year for the Flying Santa runs.

After Edward Rowe Snow's death in 1982, the Hull Lifesaving Museum took the reins. By this time, helicopters were used instead of planes, and Santa landed to greet the children at each stop. Later in the 1980s, as lighthouses were automated and destaffed, the focus began to shift to Coast Guard station visits. Friends of Flying Santa, Inc., was founded as a nonprofit organization in 1997 to continue the flights as a thank-you to Coast Guard personnel and their families. Brian Tague, president of the organization, has said, "It is a wonderful experience and helps set the mood for the Christmas season. I only wish that all those involved in making this annual event possible could have the opportunity to experience it firsthand as I have." You can learn more about the Flying Santa tradition, which currently serves more than 60 Coast Guard units from Maine to New York, at www.flyingsanta.org.

A view of Nubble Light from Flying Santa Bill Wincapaw's plane in 1937. (courtesy of Friends of Flying Santa)

December 2013. (photo by the author)

NUBBLE LIGHT, YORK BEACH, ME.

220932

NUBBLE LIGHT, NUBBLE POINT, YORK BEACH, ME.

Nubble Light, York, Me.

NUBBLE LIGHT HOUSE, YORK BEACH, ME.

(from the collection of the author)

(photo by the author)

Automation and Beyond

A crowd of more than 300 spectators witnessed an automation ceremony on July 13, 1987, watching from Sohier Park through dense fog. "It's kind of sad, but it's nice to be part of history," said the last keeper, Russ Ahlgren. At the end of the automation ceremony, Ahlgren lowered the American flag on the island one last time and presented it to Virginia Spiller, chair of the York Board of Selectmen.

News of the automation was not well received by the people of York. Local historian William O. Thomson commented to the *Wall Street Journal*, "I can't remember people getting so upset about anything since World War II broke out." The man installing the automation equipment, when asked what he was doing, avoided trouble by telling people he was going out to fix the bathroom in the keeper's house.

In 1987, Maine Senator George Mitchell, referring to the ongoing automation of lighthouses, commented, "It would be tragic if these historic structures were left to crumble." Thankfully, plenty of other people felt the same

**THE LIGHT I HAVE TENDED FOR 40 YEARS
IS NOW TO BE RUN BY A SET OF GEARS.
THE KEEPER SAID, AND IT ISN'T NICE
TO BE PUT ASHORE BY A MERE DEVICE.**

—*Edgar Guest, "The Lighthouse Keeper Wonders"*

Circa late 1980s, before the restoration of the single second-story window. (photo by the author)

way about Nubble Light. "When you think of York, you think of the Nubble," said Mike Sullivan of the town's parks and recreation department.

The Town of York started looking at options before the station was auto-

mated. The town paid an engineering firm to complete a study of the buildings at the Nubble in early 1987, and a meeting of town officials and concerned residents was held in late June 1987.

There was talk of having a caretaker,

chosen by town officials, live on the island after the Coast Guard left. It was pointed out that the house was poorly insulated, with drafty doors and windows. The old steam radiators leaked, and the roof and electrical system were in poor condition.

The Town of York was granted a 30-year lease by the Coast Guard to care for the station in 1989. In the same year, the town received a $50,000 grant from the Maine Historic Preservation Committee, along with matching funds from the town for restoration work on the keeper's house. Repairs to the roof were carried out, aluminum siding of recent vintage was replaced with cedar siding, and the gingerbread trim was restored.

When the house was first built, there was a large upstairs bedroom with a single window facing the mainland. Later, when an indoor bathroom was installed, the room was divided by a wall, and two smaller windows replaced the larger original window. As part of the restoration, the two windows were replaced by a single larger one, returning the house to its original appearance. Inside, there are still two rooms upstairs, each with half of a window.

The lighthouse tower was scraped to the bare metal in 1995 and then repainted. The project revealed that 41 coats of lead paint had been applied over the years.

June 1995 photo by H. S. Carpenter, showing the tower after the old paint had been stripped. (courtesy of Herb Carpenter)

In a 1997 article, York Parks and Recreation Director Mike Sullivan pointed out that Sohier Park was jam-packed every day and said, "Part of the allure of Nubble Light is its mystical quality. You can almost reach it, but you can't get there."

In November 1997, the people of York voted overwhelmingly to allow the town's selectmen to "adopt" the lighthouse. Under the Maine Lights Program, coordinated by the Island

(photo by the author)

ANNUAL LIGHTING OF THE NUBBLE

A display of holiday season lights at the Nubble dates to the early 1980s, when local resident Margaret Cummings donated lights in memory of her sister. Soon after the light station was automated, a popular tradition was launched—an annual holiday season lighting event for the public, held on the Saturday following Thanksgiving when strings of white lights outlining the lighthouse tower and other buildings are turned on at sunset. The lights are then turned on every evening for several weeks, through the holiday season.

The initial "Lighting of the Nubble" event in late November 1987 included carolers from York Elementary School and a brass band from the nearby town of Wells—it was so cold the instruments almost froze to their lips.

The lighting event was the brainchild of York resident Verna Rundlett, longtime Sohier Park Committee member. Before the first lighting event, her husband warned Verna that she might be disappointed with the turnout. But, as she later said, as the "magic hour" approached, she saw Sohier Park Road with "heads bobbing forth, full of eager people of all ages . . . My husband said it was like a gate suddenly opened."

Over the years, the lighting event has included music, Santa Claus, and the York Fire Department's ladder truck, among other special ingredients. Some years after the original lighting event was established, Verna Rundlett came up with the idea of a "Christmas in July" event. "We wanted to give the summer people and the snowbirds the opportunity to see what we take for granted," she said. Thousands of people now crowd into Sohier Park each summer for the event, which includes music by the Seacoast Wind Ensemble and others.

THE NUBBLE ISLAND~YORK BEACH, ME.

Institute of Rockland, the station offi-
cially became the property of the town
on June 20, 1998, at a ceremony on the
grounds of the Samoset Resort in Rockport, Maine.

At the transfer ceremony for the
Cape Neddick Light Station and more
than 20 other lighthouse properties,
Maine's Senator Olympia Snowe said,
"The transfer of these historic lights
marks a turning point for both the
Coast Guard and mariners and has become a model for lighthouses across the
country."

(from the collection of the author)

On June 28, a crowd gathered at Sohier Park to celebrate the new era for the Nubble. William O. Thompson, a beloved local historian, recounted a brief history of the lighthouse. In his speech, Mark Green, York's town manager, said, "Lighthouses have always served as a symbol of strength, independence, and most importantly, of our concern for each other. I hope that this new acquisition will help to renew and strengthen our community's commitment to these ideals."

(photo by the author)

The New Breed of Keepers

York's parks and recreation department now manages the buildings on the Nubble, along with the grounds and buildings at Sohier Park on the mainland. The light and fog signal and all equipment related to their operation are still maintained by Coast Guard aids-to-navigation personnel.

Many more improvements have been completed under the town's management in recent years, including the rebuilding of the boat ramp, the replacement of a walkway to the lighthouse, numerous repaintings of all the buildings, and the installation of an alarm system in the keeper's house.

Most repairs and the management of Sohier Park have been paid for by donations, memorial gifts, and gift shop sales. The idea of charging the public an admission fee to enter the park was discussed and rejected in 2001. Verna Rundlett of the Sohier Park Committee commented, "It's a sin to even think about it."

When the Town of York took over stewardship of the Nubble in 1989, more than 300 unsolicited applications were received from people wanting to be live-in caretakers. The town decided not to go in that direction, largely because of water and sewer issues on the island.

In 1993, 39-year-old Kent Kilgore was hired to be the chief maintenance man and caretaker at the Nubble. "This place deserves some solid attention and respect," he said. Kilgore was a physical education teacher at York Middle School for nine months out of the year, and the Nubble became his job and passion for the summer. "Look at this. It's great," he told a reporter.

One of Kilgore's pet peeves was the cigarette butts dropped on the rocks

A deer leaps over the fence in front of the keeper's house on February 19, 2013.
(Rich Beauchesne photo, 2013)

A DEER VISITS THE NUBBLE

One day in February 2013, visitors to Sohier Park were treated to the highly unusual sight of a deer on the island near the lighthouse. It wasn't clear whether the deer swam to the island or crossed the channel at low tide. Concerned for the animal's well being, two York Parks and Recreation workers waded across the channel to the island. The small doe bolted to the ocean side of the island and climbed down the rocks "like a mountain goat." It could be seen swimming to shore and reached the mainland near Short Sands Beach. The deer was later seen on shore, looking healthy.

The story became the basis of a children's book by Denise Brown of Portsmouth, New Hampshire, called *A Deer Visits Nubble Lighthouse*. "I found it irresistible to write and illustrate this story about a little deer seen running around the island and swimming ashore in the rough ocean," said Brown. "I embellished it through a deer's viewpoint and added her parent's warnings."

Damage to the keeper's house roof, sustained in the storm of April 2007, can be plainly seen in this photo taken in August 2007. (photo by the author)

by visitors. "People should just try to be more considerate," he said.

Kilgore helped improve the old trolley system, making it easier to transport equipment across the channel to the island. "Before, I had to drag the lawn mower over in the rowboat and haul it up the walkway," he said. "Now I can just send it over."

An April 2007 nor'easter damaged the keeper's house roof; both the island and Sohier Park sustained additional damage. Repairs were eventually carried out with the help of FEMA funds.

The Nubble caretaker or modern-day "keeper" for the Town of York since 2013 has been Matt Rosenberg, a teacher at York High School. He works at the Nubble and Sohier Park part time in the spring and fall, and full time in the high season of July and August.

NUBBLE LIGHT AT NIGHT, YORK BEACH, ME.

Nubble Light, York Beach, Me.

Nubble Light, York, Me.

The Nubbles, York, Me.

(from the collection of the author)

MATT ROSENBERG, 21ST-CENTURY KEEPER

With his father in the Coast Guard for 23 years, Matt Rosenberg got to experience a variety of coastal locations as he grew up, from New Jersey to Chesapeake Bay to the St. Lawrence Seaway to Lake Erie. Now a resident of Wells, Maine, and an English teacher at York High School, Matt was hired in 2013 to be the seasonal caretaker at Sohier Park and Nubble Light. His association with the location has deepened his appreciation of lighthouses. "I think they are a reminder of a different time in America's history and the values of the people who created them," he said in a 2017 interview. "Once they're gone, we can never get them back."

Matt's favorite aspect of his job as a modern-day lighthouse keeper is the people he gets to meet. "Everyone is there to have a good time, and they are usually all in a good mood. Sometimes I get to hear people's stories about their experiences at the Nubble," he has said. People often thank him for "taking care of my lighthouse," and he appreciates the fact that so many people have a close, personal connection with the location.

Matt finds little to dislike about this job, and he sees it as a privilege to care for such a beloved landmark. A pet peeve is the number of people who smoke in the park, despite no smoking signs. He spends a great deal of time picking up countless cigarette butts.

An accomplished photographer, Matt has said that he "isn't looking for a perfect sunny day or postcard-perfect vista." Instead, he's "interested in a foggy day, a broken shed door, tiny flowers and other unexpected scenes for inspiration."

During the 2016–17 school year, Matt became the mentor for a lighthouse club at York High School—the YYLPA (York Youth Lighthouse Preservation Association). The club's goal is "to spread our passion for preserving lighthouses while also involving community and volunteerism."

Matt Rosenberg, Nubble keeper.
(photo by Deb Cram)

You can read more on the official website for Nubble Light at www.nubblelight.org. On the site, you can learn the hours for the welcome center at Sohier Park, and you can make a donation to Friends of Nubble. All donations are deposited into an endowment fund and are used to preserve the physical and historical integrity of the island and park. You can also send a donation to Friends of Nubble, 186 York Street, York, Maine 03909.

Bill Thomson, the popular historian of the Nubble and the surrounding area, has written that Nubble Light doesn't seem to have any ghost stories like so many other lighthouses. He claims, however, that it is possessed by a positive energy force that leaves visitors feeling spiritually refreshed. Visit just once, and you understand that this is undeniably true.

RESTAURANTS AT THE NUBBLE

Fox's Lobster House has stood at the edge of Sohier Park with a commanding view of the Nubble since 1966. Its roots go back to 1936, when Frank and Annie Coupe opened a lobster pound restaurant on the grounds with seating for 40 people. Coupe's Lobster Pound was also known for its fried clams. The Coupes also built a smaller take-out stand in the present location of the Sohier Park welcome center. With the food shortages that came at the start of World War II, the take-out stand became a gift shop—the predecessor of today's welcome center and gift shop.

The Coupes' restaurant changed hands a couple of times, and by 1950 it became known as Brown's Lobster Pound. It was eventually bought in 1966 by Bob and Tilly Fox and their oldest son, Bob, Jr. The Foxes, who were from Dracut, Massachusetts, renamed the establishment Fox's Lobster House. It was later enlarged to seat 65 people, and a picnic patio area was added near take-out windows outside. The take-out area is always busy on nice summer days, with ice cream cones a top-selling item.

A separate establishment, the popular Nubble Restaurant and Gift Shop, stood just outside Sohier Park on Nubble Road for many years. Originally built in 1938, the restaurant was rebuilt multiple times after fires, and it was finally sold in 2004 and demolished to make room for new houses. The owners of the restaurant from 1988 to 2004 were Cheryl and Marty Flood. In a 2004 interview, Cheryl Flood said there had been quite a few marriage proposals in their dining room. She also said they had been asked many perplexing questions by friendly but confused tourists, such as, "What lake is this?" and "What time does the fog go away?"

Circa 1950s ad for the Nubble Light Dining Room. (from the collection of the author)

Circa 1950s postcard of the Nubble Restaurant. (from the collection of the author)

Circa 1969 postcard of the Nubble Restaurant. (from the collection of the author)

Circa 1980s postcard of Fox's Lobster House. (from the collection of the author)

A harbor seal on the rocks at Sohier Park, March 2016. (photo by the author)

(photo by the author)

Selected Bibliography

Caldwell, Bill. *Lighthouses of Maine*. Portland, ME: Gannett Books, 1986.

Clifford, J. Candace, and Mary Louise Clifford. *Maine Lighthouses: Documentation of Their Past*. Alexandria, VA: Cypress Communications 2005.

D'Entremont, Jeremy. *The Lighthouses of Maine*. Beverly, Massachusetts: Commonwealth Editions, 2009.

D'Entremont, Jeremy. *The Lighthouses of Maine: Southern Maine to Casco Bay*. Carlisle, Massachusetts: Commonwealth Editions, an imprint of Applewood Books, 2013.

Drake, Samuel Adams. *The Pine Tree Coast*. Boston: Estes and Lauriat, 1891.

Labrie, Rose Cushing. *Sentinel of the Sea: Nubble Light*. Hampton, NH: Hampton Publishing Company, 1958.

MacIver, Kenneth, and William Thomson. *York is Maine*. Cape Neddick, Maine: Nor'east Heritage Publications, 1983.

Patten, Jeffrey. *Cape Neddick Light Station and Sohier Park*. Undated booklet.

Porter, Jane Molloy. *Friendly Edifices: Piscataqua Lighthouses and Other Aids to Navigation, 1771-1939*. Portsmouth, NH: Peter E. Randall Publisher, 2006.

Shattuck, Clifford. *The Nubble: Cape Neddick Lightstation, York, Maine*. Freeport, ME: The Cumberland Press, Inc., 1979.

Snow, Edward Rowe. *The Lighthouses of New England*. New York: Dodd, Mead & Company, 1973.

Sterling, Robert Thayer. *Lighthouses of the Maine Coast and the Men Who Keep Them*. Brattleboro, VT: Stephen Daye Press, 1935.

Thomson, William O. *Lighthouse Legends & Hauntings*. Kennebunk, ME: 'Scapes Me, 1998.

Thomson, William O. *Nubble Light*. Published by the author, 1996.

Thomson, William O. *Nubble Light: Cape Neddick Light Station*. Kennebunk, ME: 'Scapes Me, 2000.

ONLINE SOURCES:

Ancestry.com, Newspapers.com, Newspaperarchive.com, Genealogybank.com, Boston Globe archives

New England Lighthouses: A Virtual Guide — www.newenglandlighthouses.net

Lighthouse Friends — www.lighthousefriends.com

(photo by the author)

About the Author

Jeremy D'Entremont has been involved with lighthouses for more than three decades. He has written more than a dozen books (including *The Lighthouse Handbook: New England; The Lighthouse Handbook: West Coast and All About Portland Head Light*) and hundreds of articles on lighthouses and other maritime subjects, and his photographs have appeared in countless books and magazines. He is the historian for the American Lighthouse Foundation and founder of Friends of Portsmouth Harbor Lighthouses. He has appeared on national TV and radio and has lectured on his favorite subject from Maine to California. Jeremy lives in Portsmouth, New Hampshire, with his wife, Charlotte Raczkowski, and their tuxedo cat, Evie.

(photo by the author)

Nubble Island, York Beach, Me.

York, Me., Nubble Light.

The Nubble, York Beach, Maine.

Cape Neddick.

Published in Germany by W. C. Hildreth, York Beach, Maine.

(from the collection of the author)

NUBBLE LIGHT - YORK BEACH, MAI

About Cider Mill Press
Book Publishers

Good ideas ripen with time. From seed to harvest, Cider Mill Press brings fine reading, information, and entertainment together between the covers of its creatively crafted books. Our Cider Mill bears fruit twice a year, publishing a new crop of titles each spring and fall.

"Where Good Books Are Ready for Press"

Visit us online at
cidermillpress.com

or write to us at
PO Box 454
12 Spring St.
Kennebunkport, Maine 04046